Mr D's

Recipes for the award winning Mr D's Thermal Cooker
(the slow cooker that needs no power)

3L Thermal Cookbook

by
Dave Knowles
Mr D - The Thermal Cook

Recipes from Mr D's Kitchen

Mr D's 3L Thermal Cookbook
ISBN: 978-0-9935078-5-4

Published by L:ittle Knoll Press
34 Ashleigh Close
Hythe
Hants
SO45 3QP
Tel: 023 8084 2190

First published 2009
3L Thermal Cookbook (recipes changed from the 4.5L book) 2016

Contents

Acknowledgements

To write a cookbook means hours of testing and tasting. This has been made a lot easier by the help of friends and family.

Three people who have been great help are Allan & Lindi Rush from Thermal Cookware.com in Australia, who kindly allowed me to use a number of their recipes in this book, and my good friend Mike Redcar, who most evenings has used his Thermal Cooker to try out recipes in this book.

I would like to thank my family who have eaten many Mr D's Thermal Cooker meals and given their valuable comments.

Finally a very special thanks to Jenny my wife who not only has eaten thermally cooked meals nearly every evening, but also has helped me develop many of the dishes included in this book.

Introduction

The modern thermal cooker uses the concept of the hay box, where by placing hay or straw around a cooking pot of heated food the meal continues to cook without fuel.

In the mid 1990s the thermal cooker was developed in Asia. It consisted of two pots, one within the other. The inner pot made from stainless steel was used to bring the food up to the boil and the outer, twin walled with a vacuum between the walls, was used as the container to keep the cooking process continuing.

These cookers had a particular appeal to Cantonese cooks from Guangdong in Southern China where many dishes require prolonged braising or simmering.

To use Mr D's Thermal Cooker the food is put into the inner pot and brought to the boil, and then placed in the outer pot for continued cooking.

There are a number of thermal cookers on the market. Some use insulation material between the outer pot walls, others, like Mr D's Thermal Cooker, use a vacuum.

Thermal cookers with two inner pots allow you to cook two items at the same time, such as curry and rice. All thermal cookers are capable of cooking many dishes from soups to puddings. Cakes and bread can also be cooked by partly submerging the cake/bread tin in boiling water.

The main benefits of thermal cooking

- *You only need to spend a short time preparing the food in the morning to have a hot meal later in the day. You can of course eat the meal as soon as it is cooked (normal slow cook times apply).*

- *You save up to 80% in fuel costs. Works on gas, electric and induction hobs.*

- *There is hardly any smell of cooking when using a thermal cooker*

- *The food can never be overcooked*

- *The vitamins, nutrients and flavours are kept in the pot*

- *You can adapt most slow cooker recipes to work with the thermal cooker*

- *The cooker can be taken with you and will continue cooking without power. Ideal to transport cooking food in a car, caravan, boat or motor home. You can even take it with you camping.*

Mr D's Thermal Cooker can be used as a

- *Slow cooker*

- *Portable oven*

- *Rice Cooker*

- *Bain Marie (double broiler)*

- *Cooler or Ice Bucket*

A quality thermal cooker - Mr D's 3L Thermal Cooker

Mr D's 3L Thermal Cooker consists of two containers, one inner clad stainless steel pot (for direct heating) and an outer patented vacuum-insulated container for heat preserved cooking.

INSULATED LID
removable for
easy cleaning

**INNER POT
GLASS LID**

**INNER
COOKING POT**
made from high
quality stainless
steel with a very
efficient cast iron
base

**INNER POT
HANDLES**
one piece high quality
plastic moulded onto
stainless steel brackets

**VACUUM INSULATED
OUTER CONTAINER**
made from high quality
stainless steel and the vacuum
ensures the best heat
retention.

How does it work? - Simply place your prepared ingredients in the inner pot and heat on a stove.
After it comes to the boil, let it boil for a couple of minutes to make sure it is on the boil.
Turn off heat and transfer the inner cooking pot, with the lid on, into the insulated outer container and shut the lid. That's it.
The heat is retained and your meal will continue slowly cooking for hours until you are ready to eat.

How hot will it keep food?

- Due to excellent insulation, there is only a heat loss of a few degrees per hour. This leads to the same effect as gently and slowly cooking your food for hours, but without constant attention.

After 6 hours, food in Mr D's Thermal Cooker will still have a temperature around 65 to 70°C providing the inner pot is 75 to 80% full.

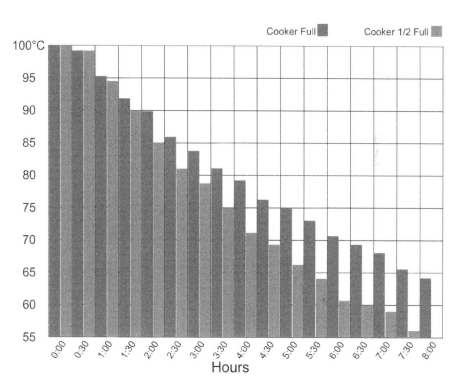

Points to remember when cooking thermally

1. The system only works effectively if there is adequate heat developed within the cooking pots and food to be cooked.
2. To last for the longest period above food safety temperature the inner cooking pot needs to be at least 75 to 80% full and to have been at boiling temperature for the required period (this is to ensure that everything within the inner pot, including the pot, has reached the highest temperature).
3. Do not freeze the inner cooking pot as it is constructed of layers dis-similar metals for maximum heat and cold retention and they will expand and contract at differing rates. However you can certainly chill the inner pot in a refrigerator.
4. You can keep foods, such as butter, cheese & cold meats, chilled for an extended period by placing ice cubes (in a sealed plastic bag) in the bottom of the inner pot and placing the food on top.

Instructions for Use

Put the inner pot on the stove or induction cooker

When the food is boiling, cover the inner pot to avoid excessive evaporation

Move the inner pot into the outer pot

Cover the outer pot to maintain heat and temperature inside

Food will continue to boil and maintain heat

Attention: After heating the inner pot, place directly into the outer pot.DO NOT place hot inner pot on any other surface in order to avoid damage, injury and accident.

Care Instructions

- Hand wash and rinse the inner cooking pot and lid thoroughly before first use and after each use.
- The outer insulated container should be wiped clean with a soft cloth dampened with warm water and mild detergent. Clean the outer pot with a damp cloth only. Never put it in water.
- Remove the lid by pressing on the clip behind the hinge. Wipe clean.
- If you do need to use a scourer use the green (made of plastic) but be aware they may dull the finish slightly.
- Do not use bleach or cleaners containing chlorine on any parts of the product.

Food Safety

Most cases of food-borne illness are due to unsafe cooking, holding or reheating temperatures. Unsafe temperatures allow harmful bacteria that might be present in food to grow. To prevent bacterial growth, maintain food at safe temperatures; 5°C or colder, or 60°C or hotter. A thermal cooker such as Mr D's Thermal Cooker can safely maintain many foods at 60°C, or hotter, for eight hours or more if you remember the following.

- Make sure that the inner pot is at least 80% full (see below "Cooking Smaller Quantities" if you are only cooking for one or two people).
- Always cook or reheat food in the thermal cooker inner cooking pot - if you transfer heated foods into the inner cooking pot restore the food to boiling temperature.
- Place the inner cooking pot into the outer insulated container only after the contents have been brought to a boil.
- Liquid foods, such as soup or sauces, can safely maintain hot temperatures longer than solid foods, such as macaroni cheese, and rice.
- If you are in a very cold environment (e.g. when camping) you can help the efficiency by warming the inside of the outer pot first with a small amount of hot water. Pour the water out and dry before putting in the inner pot.

You can safely keep liquid food hot for up to eight hours or more. The amount of food in inner pot will affect how long the food can be safely kept hot. To maximize the time it can safely keep foods hot, fill the inner cooking pot to about 2½cm from the top.

Cooking Smaller Quantities

Most of the recipes in this book can be reduced to smaller quantities and cooked using the methods below.
1. Using half or more of the ingredients, cook as instructed in the recipe. Serve within 4 hours of starting the thermal cooking, so you can be sure the food has retained a core temperature of 63 degrees or more (food safety standards).
2. Alternatively cook the smaller quantity in a lidded container such as Mr D's Top Pot (see below) and fill the main inner pot underneath it with boiling water. The water increases the volume of hot ingredients, holding food hot for longer.

Cooking Two Dishes at the Same Time

The lidded top pot from Mr D's cookware range can be used to thermal cook a second dish e.g. rice, potatoes, vegetables, or even a pudding, at the same time as the main dish.

 # Soup

There is something comforting about a bowl of soup and if it is homemade with crusty bread there is nothing quite like it on a cold winter evening. The thermal cooker is the ideal way to make soup as it cooks slowly, which helps to develop the flavours.

Due to the design of the thermal cooker all the goodness is kept in the pot and there is no danger of overcooking or drying out, even if you leave it all day or overnight.

Chicken Broth *- serves 4*

 The first part of this recipe makes an invaluable stock base for many dishes, but this clear broth is also very good just as it is, for both taste and healing qualities.

Ingredients

- 1 free range chicken (about 1.2 kg)
- 1 large onion halved
- 2 small carrots
- 2 sticks of celery, halved widthways
- 1 head of garlic , halved widthways
- 1 tsp of black peppercorns
- 1 tbsp of sea salt
- 2 fresh bay leaves
- water

For Chicken Soup

- broth from above
- coarsely shredded chicken meat from above
- 25g of butter
- 2 large onions, cut into 1 cm pieces
- 3 cloves of garlic, crushed
- 3 small leeks, white part only, cut into 1cm pieces
- 3 stalks of celery, cut into 1cm pieces
- ½ a cup of coarsely chopped flat leaf parsley
- wholemeal multigrain bread or rolls, warmed to serve

Method

1. Place all the ingredients in the inner pot and add enough water to cover the chicken.
2. Slowly bring this to the boil.
3. Let it boil for 3 or 4 minutes.
4. Turn off the heat and transfer the inner pot into the vacuum-insulated outer container.
5. Close the lid and leave to cook for a minimum of 3 hours.
6. Remove the chicken from the inner pot, strain the broth and discard the remaining solids.
7. Remove the meat from the chicken, discard the skin and bones.
8. Coarsely shred the chicken meat and save for the soup or another recipe.

Chicken Soup

1. Heat the butter in the inner pot over a low heat and add the onions, garlic, leek and celery.
2. Cook until the onion is soft.
3. Add the chicken meat and broth, slowly bring to the boil with lid on.
4. Turn off the heat and transfer the inner pot into the vacuum-insulated outer container.
5. Close the lid and leave to cook for a minimum of 2 hours. If you leave it longer it will not matter.

To serve this soup

Season to taste with sea salt and freshly ground black pepper, then stir in the parsley and serve with warmed wholemeal bread or rolls.

Garden Vegetable Soup - serves 4

 Try this great, zesty Garden Vegetable soup - great for any time of year!

Ingredients

- 1.5 litres of water
- 1 tbsp olive oil
- 2 large onions, peeled and chopped into chunks
- 1 stalk of celery, chopped into large pieces
- 2 medium carrots, peeled and diced
- 2 cloves of garlic, peeled and finely chopped
- 2 medium potatoes, peeled and diced
- 1 cup of fresh or frozen green beans
- 400g can of kidney beans, well rinsed
- 4 Roma tomatoes, diced
- 1 tbsp of basil, chopped finely
- pepper and salt to taste
- 125g of uncooked pasta noodles (optional)

Method

1. Bring the water to the boil in the inner pot.
2. Heat the olive oil in a frying pan on medium heat.
3. Stir fry the onions and celery for a minute then add the other vegetables one at a time.
4. Sprinkle with basil, pepper and salt and stir fry well for about 3 minutes.
5. Stir the cooked vegetables into the inner pot and bring the water back to the boil.
6. Put the lid on.
7. Turn off the heat and transfer the inner pot into the vacuum-insulated outer container.
8. Close the lid and leave to cook for a minimum of 2 hours. If you leave it longer it will not matter.
9. When the meal is ready to eat, bring back to the boil, add the pasta and leave to cook for 10 minutes before serving.

Thai Butternut Squash Soup - serves 4

 A soup with the taste of Thailand.

Ingredients

- 1-3 green chillies
- 7cm piece of ginger root, peeled and finely chopped
- 2-3 lemongrass sticks - just the soft middle part finely chopped
- 1 handful of coriander stalks - keep the leaves for garnish
- 1½ tsp of Chinese five spice
- 1 tsp ground cumin
- 2 tbsp olive oil
- 1 onion, sliced
- 1 small butternut squash (around 1kg peeled), deseed and chop into 2½cm cubes
- 600ml vegetable stock
- 400g can of coconut milk
- 2 limes
- salt and pepper.

Method

1. Make a paste out of the first six ingredients in a food processor or pestle and mortar.
2. Put the olive oil in the inner pot and heat on medium heat.
3. Add the paste and the sliced onion to the inner pot and cook for about 5 minutes until the onion is soft.
4. Add the squash and stock. Bring to the boil.
5. Boil for 3 minutes.
6. Add the coconut milk, juice of limes, 1tsp of salt and a good pinch of pepper.
7. Bring back to the boil and let it boil for 3 or 4 minutes.
8. Put on the lid, turn off the heat and transfer the inner pot into the vacuum-insulated outer container.
9. Close the lid and leave to cook for a minimum of 2 hours. If you leave it longer it will not matter.
10. Before serving blend the soup with a hand blender or in a liquidiser, and check the seasoning, adding a little more salt if needed.

To serve this soup

Serve garnished with chopped coriander leaves.

Sweet Potato Soup - serves 4

 A sweet wholesome soup.

Ingredients

- 15ml of olive oil
- 2 cloves of garlic, crushed
- 1 medium onion, coarsely chopped
- 700g sweet potatoes, peeled and chopped
- 1 red pepper, deseeded and chopped
- 725ml vegetable stock
- 150ml coconut milk
- salt and pepper

Method

1. Put the inner pot on medium heat and add the olive oil and garlic.
2. Heat gently, stirring occasionally to make sure the garlic does not burn.
3. Add the onions and cook until they are soft.
4. Add the sweet potato and pepper and cook, occasionally stirring, for 5 minutes.
5. Add the stock and bring to the boil.
6. Boil for 3 minutes.
7. Add the coconut milk, 1tsp of salt and a good pinch of pepper. Stir well.
8. Bring back to the boil and let it boil for 3 or 4 minutes.
9. Put on the lid, turn off the heat and transfer the inner pot into the vacuum-insulated outer container.
10. Close the lid and leave to cook for a minimum of 2 hours. If you leave it longer it will not matter.
11. Before serving blend the soup with a hand blender or in a liquidiser, and check the seasoning, adding a little more salt if needed.

Pumpkin Soup - serves 6 to 8

 This is a creamy, rich soup with a deliciously rich colour.

Ingredients

- 40g of butter
- 2 tbsp of olive oil
- 2 diced onions
- 3 cloves of garlic
- 3 rashers of bacon, trimmed and diced
- water
- 1 kg pumpkin, peeled and cut into fairly large chunks
- 1 vegetable stock cube
- 6 stalks of parsley
- 125ml of milk or coconut milk
- salt and pepper to taste
- sour cream for garnish
- chopped chives for garnish

Method

1. Gently fry the onions, garlic and bacon in the butter and olive oil in the inner pot over a medium heat.
2. Turn the heat down and add the pumpkin and enough boiling water to fill the inner pot to 75-80%, then add the stock cube, parsley, salt and pepper.
3. Bring back to the boil and let it boil for 3 or 4 minutes.
4. Put on the lid, turn off the heat and transfer the inner pot into the vacuum-insulated outer container.
5. Close the lid and leave to cook for a minimum of 1 hour. If you leave it longer it will not matter.
6. Remove the inner pot and puree the soup with milk or coconut milk.

To serve this soup

Check the seasoning and adjust if needed. Garnish with the sour cream and chopped chives.

Carrot & Ginger Soup *- serves 6*

 This is a recipe given to me in 1993 by Alasdair Junor, Club Manager at the Al Falah Club Abu Dhabi.

Ingredients

- 40g of butter
- 400g of carrots, cut into cubes
- 5 cm piece of ginger, peeled and sliced
- 100g onions, chopped
- 2 litres of either vegetable or beef stock
- 500 ml of cream
- salt and pepper to taste

Method

1. Put the inner pot over a medium heat, add the butter and let it melt.
2. Add the carrots, ginger and onions and cook for around 2 minutes stirring occasionally.
3. Add the stock and bring to the boil and let it boil for 3 or 4 minutes.
4. Put on the lid, turn off the heat and transfer the inner pot into the vacuum-insulated outer container.
5. Close the lid and leave to cook for a minimum of 1 hour. If you leave it longer it will not matter.
6. When ready, remove the inner pot and use either in a liquidiser or hand blender to blitz the contents until smooth.
7. Add the cream and put the inner pot back on the heat until it just comes back to the boil, stirring all the time.
8. Check for seasoning and add salt and pepper as required.

Cauliflower & Cheese Soup *- serves 4 to 6*

 A delicious soup, fit for a dinner party.

Ingredients

- 1 medium head of cauliflower, separated into florets
- 1 medium onion, chopped
- 1 carrot, chopped
- 1 stick of celery, chopped
- 1 litre vegetable stock
- ½ tsp Worcestershire sauce
- 1 cup mature Cheddar cheese, grated
- salt and pepper
- 2 cups light cream
- chopped chives

Method

1. Put the cauliflower, onion, carrot, celery and vegetable stock into the inner pot.
2. Bring to the boil and let it boil for 3 or 4 minutes.
3. Put on the lid, turn off the heat and transfer the inner pot into the vacuum-insulated outer container.
4. Close the lid and leave to cook for a minimum of 2 hours. If you leave it longer it will not matter.
5. Remove the inner pot and blend the contents to a smooth consistency.
6. Add the cream, Worcestershire sauce and cheese.
7. Add salt and pepper to taste.
8. Stir well and heat up if needed.

To serve this soup
Serve in bowls garnished with chopped chives.

Tomato & Tamarind Soup - serves 4

 This is based on South Indian Rasam. It makes a great soup to have before an Indian meal.

Ingredients

- groundnut or vegetable oil
- ½ tsp mustard seed
- 1 tsp cumin seed
- ½ tsp chilli powder
- ¼ tsp ground black pepper
- ½ tsp salt
- 2 tbsp tomato puree
- 2 garlic cloves, minced
- a thumb-sized piece root ginger, minced
- 1 tbsp tamarind paste
- a small bunch coriander, stalks and leaves chopped and separated
- 2 x 400g tins chopped tomatoes
- 3 cups of vegetable stock
- 1 cup of yellow lentils
- 4 tbsp natural yoghurt

Method

1. Heat 1 tbsp of oil in the inner pot.
2. Add the mustard seeds and cumin seeds. Let them splutter.
3. Turn down the heat to medium and add the chilli powder, ground pepper, salt, tomato puree, garlic and ginger. Cook for 2 minutes.
4. Add the tamarind paste, chopped coriander stalks, tins of tomatoes, vegetable stock and lentils.
5. Bring to the boil and let it boil for 3 or 4 minutes.
6. Put on the lid, turn off the heat and transfer the inner pot into the vacuum-insulated outer container.
7. Close the lid and leave to cook for a minimum of 1 hour. If you leave it longer it will not matter.

To serve this soup

Check the seasoning and adjust if needed. To serve, blend until smooth. Then mix together the yoghurt and coriander leaves before swirling it into the soup.

Porcini Mushroom Soup - serves 4 to 6

 After a busy day curl up with a bowl of mushroom soup in the evening - just heaven.

Ingredients

- 1.5 litres of vegetable stock
- ½ tsp saffron threads
- 2 tbsp olive oil
- 6 tbsp minced shallots
- 2 tbsp finely chopped garlic
- 100g dried porcini mushrooms, soaked and sliced
- 185g ounces white mushrooms, sliced
- ⅛ tsp curry powder
- 60g finely diced peeled carrot
- 60g finely diced peeled potato
- 2 tbsp butter
- Salt and pepper to taste

Method

1. Soak the porcini mushrooms in 500ml of hot stock for about 15 minutes, or until they are soft.
2. Add the saffron to 50ml of hot stock and leave to one side for later.
3. Heat the oil in the inner pot over medium heat.
4. Add shallots and garlic, stir 1 minute.
5. Add the curry powder and white mushrooms. Sauté until mushrooms release liquid.
6. Pour in the saffron mixture and porcini mushrooms with the water they have been soaking in.
7. Add the diced carrot and potato and the rest of the stock.
8. Bring to the boil and let it boil for 3 or 4 minutes.
9. Put on the lid, turn off the heat and transfer the inner pot into the vacuum-insulated outer container.
10. Close the lid and leave to cook for a minimum of 1 hour. If you leave it longer it will not matter.

To serve this soup
Check the seasoning and adjust if needed. You may like to try this topped with freshly grated Parmesan

Middle Eastern Soup - serves 6

 This is a wonderful soup with fragrance of the Middle East. It is perfect food for serving with warm pita bread straight from the oven.

Ingredients

- 3 tbsp groundnut oil
- 225g onion, finely chopped
- 5 cloves garlic
- 175g finely chopped lamb
- 3 tsp chilli powder
- 2 tsp cumin powder
- 2 tsp coriander powder
- 1 tsp allspice, ground
- 150g tomato puree
- 1 green chilli, deseeded and finely chopped
- 1.25 litre of hot lamb stock
- 1 tsp black pepper
- 2 tsp sugar
- 2 tsp salt
- 1 tbsp dried mint
- 2 preserved lemons, chopped into small pieces
- 400g can of chick peas

Method

1. Heat the oil in the inner pot, add the onion and garlic and cook until they are lightly browned.
2. Add the finely chopped meat and cook, stirring frequently until the pieces of meat are all lightly browned.
3. Turn the heat down, stir in the ground spices (chilli powder, cumin, coriander and allspice) and cook for 1 minute.
4. Add the tomato puree and fresh chilli.
5. Mix everything together and add the stock then the pepper, sugar, salt, dried mint, lemon (juice and skin) and drained chick peas.
6. Bring to the boil and let it boil for 3 or 4 minutes.
7. Put on the lid, turn off the heat and transfer the inner pot into the vacuum-insulated outer container.
8. Close the lid and leave to cook for a minimum of 1 hour. If you leave it longer it will not matter.

To serve this soup

Check the seasoning and adjust if needed. Serve in bowls with warm pita bread.

PRESERVED LEMONS:
These are available in many supermarkets. They add a tang and saltiness to many Mediterranean dishes. If you want to make your own go to basic recipes page 106.

 # Mains Poultry

Poultry cooked in a thermal cooker keeps moist and tender. Poultry if cooked for a long time will just fall off the bones.

Poached Herb Chicken – serves 4 to 6

 Herbed chicken and vegetables...what more can you say.....just enjoy.

Ingredients

- **1.2kg chicken**
- **1 bunch assorted fresh herbs of your choice**
- **1 tsp of olive oil**
- **1 medium white onion, peeled and coarsely chopped**
- **3 large carrots, peeled and cut into quarters**
- **8 small red potatoes, well scrubbed but not peeled**
- **1.5 litres of chicken stock**
- **1 tsp of salt**
- **9 whole black peppercorns**
- **2 cups of fresh green beans**
- **¼ cup of Dijon mustard**
- **3 tbsp of cornflour**

Method

1. Stuff the chicken with the herbs and put it in the fridge.
2. Heat the inner pot on medium heat, add the olive oil and onions and fry for about 3 minutes.
3. Add the carrots and fry for another 2 minutes.
4. Place the chicken (whole if small or cut into quarters if medium size) on the onions and carrots.
5. Tuck the potatoes around the chicken and pour the stock over.
6. Add the salt and peppercorns.
7. Bring to the boil skimming off any foam that rises to the surface.
8. Place the green beans and herbs on top of the chicken pieces, bring back to the boil and let it boil for 3 or 4 minutes.
9. Put on the lid, turn off the heat and transfer the inner pot into the vacuum-insulated outer container.
10. Close the lid and leave to cook for a minimum of 4 hours. If you leave it longer it will not matter.

Before serving the meal make the sauce
1. Take 3 cups of the hot chicken stock from the pot, strain off the fat and pour into a saucepan.
2. Remove ½ a cup of this liquid and mix it with the mustard and cornflour to make a paste.
3. Stir the paste into the stock. Put the pan on a gentle heat and keep stirring until it thickens.
4. When suitably thickened, turn off the heat.

To serve the meal
Remove the chicken from the pot and slice it thinly. Serve the chicken with the potatoes and green beans and pour the sauce over the top.

Thai Green Chicken Curry - serves 4

 A delightfully mild chicken curry with the fresh Thai flavour.

Ingredients

- 1 tbsp of oil
- 500g of sliced chicken fillets
- 3 tbsp of green curry paste (you can increase or decrease the amount of curry paste to suit your own requirements)
- 400ml tin of coconut cream
- 2 tbsp of fish sauce
- 2 tsp of sugar
- 1 cup of chopped pumpkin
- 1 cup of green beans
- 1 cup of fresh basil leaves, chopped
- 2 kaffir lime leaves or 1 cup of freshly chopped coriander
- salt & pepper
- 2 cups fragrant rice (Jasmine) to serve

Method

1. In the inner pot stir-fry the curry paste in the oil over low heat until fragrant.
2. Add the chicken and pumpkin then stir-fry over medium heat for a few minutes.
3. Add the remaining ingredients, lower the heat, slowly bring it to the boil and let it boil for 3 or 4 minutes.
4. Put on the lid, turn off the heat and transfer the inner pot into the vacuum-insulated outer container.
5. Close the lid and leave to cook for a minimum of 2 hours. If you leave it longer it will not matter.

To serve the meal

Check seasoning and add salt if required before serving on a bed of fragrant steamed rice which you can cook in a Mr D's Top Pot (see page 103) if you have one.

Chicken in Chinese Master Stock - serves 6

 This recipe uses the master stock which appears on page 98. This unusual way of cooking gives the chicken a real oriental taste that is great when eaten hot or cold.

Ingredients

- the master stock from page 98
- 1.2kg chicken

Method

1. Place the chicken in the inner pot of the thermal cooker.
2. Pour over the master stock, making sure the bird is covered.
3. Bring to the boil and boil for 3 to 4 minutes.
4. Put on the lid, turn off the heat and transfer the inner pot into the vacuum-insulated outer container.
5. Close the lid and leave to cook for a minimum of 4 hours. If you leave it longer it will not matter.

To serve the meal

Serve hot with rice and stir-fry vegetables, or leave to get cold and eat the chicken with salad or in sandwiches.

Poached Guinea Fowl - serves 4 to 6

 A guinea fowl cooked this way will keep wonderfully moist. A complete meal ideal for an evening with friends.

Ingredients

- a guinea fowl
- 2 carrots, washed and cut into 2 to 3cm slices
- 1 medium leek, cleaned and cut into 5cm lengths
- 1 fennel bulb, cut in half
- 2 celery sticks, halved
- 10 small potatoes, washed but not peeled
- 1 bay leaf
- water
- vegetable stock cube
- salt and freshly ground pepper

Method

1. Wash the guinea fowl and place it into the inner pot.
2. Add the carrots and leeks to the pot.
3. Add the two halves of fennel bulb, celery and potatoes.
4. Add the bay leaf, enough water to cover all the ingredients in the pot and mix in the stock cube.
5. Bring to the boil and boil for 3 to 4 minutes.
6. Put on the lid, turn off the heat and transfer the inner pot into the vacuum-insulated outer container.
7. Close the lid and leave to cook for a minimum of 4 hours. If you leave it longer it will not matter.

To serve the meal

Check the stock for seasoning and carve the guinea fowl, spooning some of the stock over the guinea fowl and placing the vegetables around the side..

Chicken Adobo - serves 4 to 6

This is a Filipino dish and adobo refers to the very popular cooking process of stewing with vinegar. Typically, chicken, pork, or a combination of both, are slowly cooked in soy sauce and vinegar which inhibits the growth of bacteria. The standard accompaniment to adobo is white rice.

Ingredients

- 6 garlic cloves, crushed
- olive oil or vegetable oil
- 1tsp of ground black pepper
- 3 bay leaves
- 3 birdseye chillies
- 400ml of rice vinegar
- 200ml of soy sauce
- 1 chicken, cut into eight pieces

Method

1. Combine all the ingredients into a non metal container or casserole dish.
2. Make sure that the chicken is coated by the liquid and put the container in the fridge for a minimum of 2 hours, but preferably overnight.
3. After minimum of two hours or preferably overnight remove the chicken from the fridge and put the marinade and chicken in the inner pot of the thermal cooker.
4. Bring to the boil and boil for 3 to 4 minutes.
5. Put on the lid, turn off the heat and transfer the inner pot into the vacuum-insulated outer container.
6. Close the lid and leave to cook for a minimum of 3 hours. If you leave it longer it will not matter.

To serve the meal
Check seasoning and add salt if required before serving on a bed of fragrant steamed rice which you can cook in a Mr D's Top Pot (see page 103) if you have one.

Chicken Loaf - serves 4 to 6

 An excellent meal served sliced cold with salad or even with biscuits and cheese.

Ingredients

- 350g of chicken mince
- ¼ cup of shelled pistachio nuts
- 250g of pork mince
- 2 tbsp of chopped parsley
- 3 rashers of bacon, finely chopped
- ½ cup of fresh bread crumbs
- 2 tbsp tinned green peppercorns
- 2 tsp of brandy (optional)
- 4 shallots, finely sliced
- 1 large egg
- 1 clove of garlic, crushed
- salt and freshly ground black pepper

Method

1. Place baking paper onto the bottom of a loaf tin* or other suitable container that will fit the inner pot. Ensure that the container is wider rather than deeper. You will also need a trivet to support the tin inside the inner pot.
2. Pour the brandy over the breadcrumbs.
3. Whisk the egg and add this to the breadcrumbs.
4. Combine all the ingredients together in a large bowl, mixing well with a wooden spoon or clean hands.
5. Place the mixture into the loaf tin and pat down firmly.
6. Cover the tin with foil or if using the steamed loaf tin the lid.
7. Place the tin inside the inner pot on a trivet.
8. Carefully pour hot water into the inner pot so that the level comes to ¾ the height of the loaf tin.
9. Bring to the boil.
10. Turn the heat down and simmer gently for 20 minutes with the lid on.
11. Turn off the heat and transfer the inner pot into the vacuum-insulated outer container.
12. Close the lid and leave to cook for a minimum of 2 hours. If you leave it longer it will not matter.
13. The loaf can be served hold or cold.

* A Mr D's Loaf Tin with lid is available from www.MrDsCookware.com. See the back of the recipe book for details.

Jambalaya *- serves 4 to 6*

A Louisiana Creole dish of Spanish and French influence. The ingredients can be changed to suit what is available.

Ingredients

- 1.5kg whole chicken
- 1 tsp of olive oil
- 125g of bacon, sliced into approximately 2 cm pieces
- 3 medium onions, peeled and chopped into large chunks
- 3 cloves of garlic, peeled and crushed
- 1 red capsicum, seeded and chopped into 2 cm cubes
- 1 yellow capsicum, seeded, chopped into 2 cm cubes
- 3 medium carrots, peeled and finely sliced
- 2 sticks of celery, finely chopped
- 1 tbsp of chilli powder
- ½ tbsp of crushed cayenne pepper or paprika
- 1½ cups of long-grain white rice
- ½ cup of tomato paste
- 3 cups of ham stock
- 1 tin chopped tomatoes
- ½ tsp of crushed black pepper
- ½ cup of minced parsley
- 1 bay leaf
- 1 bunch of fresh spinach leaves, washed and cut into fine shreds

Method

1. Cut the legs, thighs and breast off the chicken, remove the skin and bones, then cut the meat into large chunks and set this aside. The chicken bones can be used for a stock for other meals later.
2. Lightly brown the chicken in the inner pot then remove it and place it aside for later.
3. Pour the olive oil into the saucepan and add the bacon and brown it on all sides.
4. Stir in the onions and garlic, and cook for 2 minutes.
5. Add the capsicums, carrots, celery, chilli powder and cayenne (or paprika), and stir until all the vegetables are coated with the spices.
6. Add the rest of the ingredients except the spinach.
7. Bring to the boil and boil for 3 to 4 minutes.
8. Put on the lid, turn off the heat and transfer the inner pot into the vacuum-insulated outer container.
9. Close the lid and leave to cook for a minimum of 3 hours.

To serve the meal

Spread the spinach shreds over each plate to form a crisp green nest, then spoon the hot Jambalaya onto this nest.

Kari Ayam (Malay Chicken Curry) - serves 4

A lovely aromatic Malaysian recipe that can be altered by the amount & heat of the curry powder used.

Ingredients

- 2 onions, 1 chopped and 1 sliced
- 2 garlic cloves
- 1 x 2.5cm piece fresh root ginger
- 1 chicken stock cube
- 8 boned skinless chicken thighs
- 2 tbsp groundnut oil
- 1 tsp ground cinnamon
- 2 cloves
- 1 star anise
- 3 tsp curry powder, mixed with a little water to form paste
- 400g can coconut milk
- water
- 8 small potatoes, un-peeled and halved
- salt and pepper

Method

1. Grind the chopped onion, ginger, garlic and stock cube to a smooth paste using a pestle and mortar or a food processor.
2. Rub the chicken with the onion paste and leave to marinate in the fridge for about 1 hour.
3. Heat the oil in the inner pot, add the sliced onion, cinnamon, cloves and star anise. Fry for a couple of minutes over a medium heat.
4. Add the curry paste and fry for another 3 minutes.
5. Put the chicken and marinade into the inner pot.
6. Seal the chicken all over.
7. Add the potatoes, coconut milk, 1 teaspoon of salt and water to cover the chicken by about 5 cms.
8. Bring the contents to the boil and give them a stir.
9. Boil for 3 to 4 minutes.
10. Put on the lid, turn off the heat and transfer the pot into the vacuum-insulated outer container.
11. Close the lid and leave to cook for a minimum of 2 hours. If you leave it longer it will not matter.

To serve the meal
Adjust the seasoning if needed and serve with rice which you can cook in a Mr D's Top Pot (see page 103) if you have one.

Braised Chicken - serves 4

 Braising is the ideal way of cooking chicken. Because the chicken sits in the cooking liquid it absorbs all the flavours and keeps it moist.

Ingredients

- 4 chicken quarters, legs separated from the thighs
- 2 tbsp olive oil
- 1 glass of red wine
- 2 cloves of garlic crushed
- 1 small sprig of thyme
- 8 shallots quartered
- 500ml of chicken stock
- 18 button mushrooms, quartered
- 20 green olives, pitted
- 400g can of chopped tomatoes
- 20 basil leaves

Method

1. Add the olive oil to the inner pot and heat.
2. Season the chicken and put into the heated inner pot.
3. Lightly brown the chicken in the inner pot then remove it and place it aside for later.
4. Brown the shallots in the pot.
5. Add the wine and simmer to reduce it to half.
6. Add the chicken, garlic, thyme and stock. Top up with some water if necessary to cover the chicken.
7. Bring the contents to the boil and give them a stir.
8. Boil for 3 to 4 minutes.
9. Put on the lid, turn off the heat and transfer the inner pot into the vacuum-insulated outer container.
10. Close the lid and leave to cook for a minimum of 1 hour.
11. Just before serving, cook some pasta such as linguine.

To serve the meal
Divide the pasta into four bowls. Put one piece of chicken on top of the pasta. Strain the sauce and pour it over the chicken and pasta. Put some olives, chopped tomatoes and basil leaves around the chicken pieces.

Coq au Vin *- serves 4 to 6*

 A little bit of France captured in a thermal cooker.

Ingredients

- **1.5kg of chicken pieces wings and legs on the bones**
- **3 slices of bacon**
- **4 spring onions, chopped**
- **4 small onions, sliced**
- **olive oil for frying**
- **250g of button mushrooms**
- **2 cloves of garlic, crushed**
- **1 tbsp of dried thyme**
- **8 small potatoes, scrubbed and halved**
- **1 cup of red wine**
- **1 cup of chicken stock**
- **a small bunch of parsley, finely chopped**

Method

1. Fry the chicken pieces in the inner pot until well browned on all sides.
2. Remove the chicken pieces and place them to one side.
3. In the same pan brown the bacon and spring onions and then remove them to one side.
4. Place the onions, mushrooms and garlic into the inner pot.
5. Add the chicken, bacon, spring onion, thyme, potatoes, wine, stock, salt and pepper to taste.
6. Bring the contents to the boil and give them a stir.
7. Boil for 3 to 4 minutes.
8. Put on the lid, turn off the heat and transfer the inner pot into the vacuum-insulated outer container.
9. Close the lid and leave to cook for a minimum of 1 hour. If you leave it longer it will not matter.

Chicken Wings - serves 4 to 6

 A popular Chinese dish for sharing.

Ingredients

- 12 chicken wings
- Soy sauce for marinade
- 2 tbsp vegetable oil
- 4 or 5 spring onions, sliced into 1 cm pieces
- 2 cm piece ginger, peeled and sliced
- 60ml chicken stock
- 3 tbsp oyster sauce
- 2 tbsp soy sauce
- 1 tbsp Sugar
- 2 tbsp Shaoxing Chinese rice wine

Method

1. Marinate the chicken wings in soy sauce for 20 minutes.
2. Add oil to inner pot and fry the chicken wings over medium heat.
3. Remove the wings and keep warm.
4. Add the ginger and spring onions and fry for a couple of minutes.
5. Add the stock, oyster sauce, soy sauce, sugar and wine, and bring to the boil.
6. Add the chicken wings, stir-cook over medium heat for 5 minutes.
7. Turn off the heat put the lid on and transfer the inner pot into the vacuum-insulated outer container.
8. Close the lid and leave to cook for a minimum of 20 to 30 minutes. If you leave it longer it will not matter.
9. Before serving, put the inner pot back on the heat with the lid removed and cook until the sauce thickens.

Mains Seafood

The gentle cooking of a thermal cooker is ideal for seafood. Fish will not disintegrate during cooking but you do need to cook it for a shorter time than meat. It will cook in about the same time as rice or pasta, so is ideal when combined with these in a one-pot meal.

Steamed Fish - serves 4

 This meal is so quick and is deliciously healthy, light and definitely good for you.

Ingredients

- **500g of firm-flesh fish fillets**
- **2 tbsp soy sauce**
- **2 tsp sesame oil**
- **Salt and pepper to taste**
- **½ cup of finely sliced shallots**

You will need a steamer/top pot (see page 112) that fits into the inner pot for this recipe.

Alternatively: You could replace the soy sauce and sesame oil with lemon juice or use any of your choice of marinades

---

Method

1. Cut a round of baking paper to line the base of the stainless steel steamer/top pot.
2. Lay the pieces of fish on the baking paper.
3. Baste the fish with the soy sauce, sesame oil, salt and pepper.
4. Sprinkle with the sliced shallots.
5. Fill the inner pot with enough boiling water so that it is not quite in contact with the base of the steamer/top pot.
6. Place the steamer/top pot inside the inner pot on a trivet.
7. Steam over simmering water with the lid on for 3 minutes.
8. Turn off the heat and transfer the inner pot into the vacuum-insulated outer container.
9. Close the lid and leave to cook for a minimum of 30 minutes. If you leave it little longer it will not matter but not too long or the fish will be very overcooked.

To serve the meal
Check seasoning and add salt if required. Serve with a freshly tossed green salad or on a bed of fragrant steamed rice.

Seafood Paella - serves 4 to 6

 A delightful rich meal that is usually time consuming to cook, but with the Shuttle Chef it is so simple and rewarding.

Ingredients

- ½ tsp of saffron threads
- 2 tbsp olive oil
- 1 large onion, finely chopped
- 2 cloves of garlic, crushed
- 2 medium ripe tomatoes, chopped
- 1 cup of Arborio rice
- 500ml fish stock or chicken stock
- ½ cup frozen or dried peas
- 1 tsp of smoked paprika
- Salt and pepper to taste
- 500g mixed seafood
- 8 small black mussels in their shells, scrubbed and debearded

Method

1. Add the saffron threads to 2 tablespoons of boiling water, stir and leave to soak for 10 minutes.
2. Heat the oil in the inner pot and sauté the onions over a low-medium heat until soft.
3. Add the garlic and tomatoes and cook over a medium heat until the tomatoes are thick and pulpy.
4. Add the rice and stir to coat with the mixture.
5. Stir in the hot stock, peas, paprika, salt and pepper. Bring the mixture to a simmer.
6. Gently stir in the mixed seafood.
7. Add the mussels and push them into the mixture. Close the lid.
8. Simmer for 1 minute.
9. Turn off the heat and transfer the inner pot into the vacuum-insulated outer container.
10. Close the lid and leave to cook for a minimum of 45 minutes. If you leave it little longer it will not matter but not too long or the mussels will be very overcooked.
11. Once cooked, discard any mussels that failed to open and serve.

Lemon Grass Fish on Rice - serves 4

 The fish is cooked on the rice in this dish.

Ingredients

- 1½ cups jasmine rice
- 2½ cups water
- 4 firm white fish fillets

Marinade

- 2 lemon grass stems
- ½ cup chopped fresh coriander
- 1 tsp grated ginger
- 3 cloves garlic, crushed
- 4 spring onions, sliced thinly
- ½ tsp finely chopped chilli
- 1 lime, thinly sliced

Method

1. Cut the lemon grass in half lengthways and trim into 10 cm lengths.
2. Combine marinade ingredients in a small bowl and spread evenly over the fish fillets. Leave in the fridge for 30 minutes.
3. Wash rice and place in inner pot with 2½ cups of water.
4. Bring the rice to the boil. When boiling stir with a fork to break up any lumps.
5. Place the marinated fish on the rice with the lime slices on the top.
6. Put on the lid, turn off the heat and transfer the inner pot into the vacuum-insulated outer container.
7. Close the lid and leave to cook for a minimum of 30 minutes. If you leave it little longer it will not matter but not too long or the fish will be very overcooked.

Coconut Curried Fish - serves 4

 A tasty and easy one dish meal with the influence of the Far East. Nice served with steamed white rice.

Ingredients

- 6 shallots, finely chopped
- 6 cloves garlic, crushed
- 2 lemon grass stalks, finely chopped
- 4 small fresh chillies, deseeded and finely chopped
- 4 Kaffir lime leaves
- 1 small tsp tomato paste
- 1 tsp brown sugar
- 2 tbsp fish sauce
- 1 small bunch fresh basil, chopped
- 400ml can coconut milk
- ½ cup water
- 750g firm white fish, cut into chunks

Method

1. Place all ingredients except the fish into the inner pot and bring to the boil.
2. Turn the heat down and simmer very gently for 2 minutes.
3. Add fish to pot and continue to simmer, very gently with lid on for 3 minutes.
4. Turn off the heat and transfer the inner pot into the vacuum-insulated outer container.
5. Close the lid and leave to cook for a minimum of 20 minutes. If you leave it little longer it will not matter but not too long or the fish will be very overcooked.

To serve the meal

Check seasoning and add salt if required before serving on a bed of fragrant steamed rice which you can cook in a Mr D's Top Pot (see page 103) if you have one.

Poached Fish - serves 4

 Trout or salmon could be substituted for the white fish if you fancy something different.

Ingredients

- **4 firm white fish fillets**

Stock
- **750ml water**
- **4 tbsp white wine vinegar**
- **1 carrot, sliced**
- **1 onion, sliced**
- **1 bay leaf**
- **1 sprig thyme**
- **A few stalks of parsley**
- **1 tsp black peppercorns**
- **salt**

Method

1. Place all stock ingredients in inner pot and bring to the boil.
2. Boil uncovered for 3 minutes.
3. Put the lid on and continue boiling for 2 minutes.
4. Turn off the heat and transfer the inner pot into the vacuum-insulated outer container.
5. Close the lid and leave to cook for 30 minutes.
6. Strain the stock and bring back to boil.
7. Reduce heat so that stock is just simmering. Place fish into stock and put on the lid.
8. Gently simmer for 3 minutes.
9. Turn off the heat and transfer the inner pot into the vacuum-insulated outer container.
10. Close the lid and leave to cook for a minimum of 20 minutes. If you leave it little longer it will not matter but not too long or the fish will be very overcooked.

Mains Lamb

Lamb features prominently in Mediterranean, Asian and the Middle Eastern cooking. The slow cooking of the thermal cooker is ideal for the tagines of Morocco and curries of India. As for lamb shanks, the meat just falls off the bone when slowly cooked in a thermal cooker.

Navarin of Lamb - serves 4

 Tender lamb and vegetables in a rich wine gravy makes this classic French casserole a delicious meal.

Ingredients

- 1kg leg of lamb or mutton, cut into 2cm cubes
- Seasoned flour
- 30g of butter
- 2 tbsp olive oil
- 10 shallots, peeled
- 1 to 2 cloves of garlic
- 2 carrots, chopped into bite size pieces
- 2 small parsnips, cut into bite sized pieces
- 2 sticks of celery, cut into bite sized pieces
- 2 small potatoes
- 12 fresh green beans, topped and tailed
- 2 tbsp tomato paste
- 2 tsp Dijon mustard
- 750ml of chicken stock
- 250ml of dry white wine
- 1 bouquet garni (small bunch of fresh herbs, thyme, parsley and bay leaf)

Method

1. Coat the meat with the seasoned flour.
2. Heat the oil and butter into the inner pot of your thermal cooker.
3. Add the meat in batches to the inner pot and brown it in the oil and butter. Cook in two or three batches so it browns and does not stew.
4. When browned, remove the meat and add the garlic, making sure that it doesn't burn.
5. Add all the vegetables and fry for 2 to 3 minutes.
6. Add the tomato paste and mustard.
7. Return the meat to the hot pot.
8. Add the stock, wine and bouquet garni. If the meat and vegetables are not covered, add water or more stock.
9. Bring to the boil and boil for 3 to 4 minutes.
10. Put on the lid, turn off the heat and transfer the inner pot into the vacuum-insulated outer container.
11. Close the lid and leave to cook for a minimum of 3 hours. If you leave it longer it will not matter.

To serve the meal

When cooked, serve with crusty bread.

Lamb Machboos - serves 4

 This recipe was given to me by the chef for the Etihad lounge at Abu Dhabi airport.

Ingredients

Baharat spice mix
- ¾ tsp coriander
- ¾ tsp cinnamon
- ¾ tsp cloves
- 1½ tsp paprika
- 1½ tsp cardamom
- ¼ tsp nutmeg
- 1 tsp cumin
- 1 tsp black pepper

Main ingredients
- 1 kg leg of lamb or mutton, cut into 2cm cubes
- 2 tbsp ghee or vegetable oil
- 2 onions, chopped
- 1 lemon peel, removed and cut into thin strips
- 2 cloves garlic, chopped
- 200g tomatoes, chopped
- 1 litre of water
- Salt
- ⅛ tsp saffron
- 2 cups basmati rice

Cucumber Yoghurt
- ½ cucumber, finely chopped
- 1 tsp of salt
- 1 small garlic clove, crushed
- ¼ tsp grated ginger
- 1 cup of yoghurt
- lemon juice to taste

Pita bread

Method

1. Grind the Baharat spices together in either a pestle and mortar or an electric grinder and save it for later.
2. Rub the lamb with salt.
3. Heat the ghee in the thermal cooker inner pot over a medium heat.
4. Add the onions, lemon rind and garlic. Cook slowly until the onions are soft but not browned.
5. Add the lamb. Cook until lightly browned.
6. Add the Baharat spice mix, stirring well so the meat is nicely coated.
7. Stir in the tomatoes.
8. Add the water and saffron.
9. Add the salt and bring to the boil and boil for 3 to 4 minutes.
10. Add the rice stirring it gently into the liquid above the lamb. Replace the lid. (It is important to keep the lamb as a layer under the rice).
11. Turn off the heat and transfer the inner pot into the vacuum-insulated outer container.
12. Close the lid and leave to cook for a minimum of 2 hours. If you leave it longer it will not matter.
13. For the cucumber yoghurt put the cucumber in a bowl, sprinkle with salt and place in the fridge.
14. When the lamb is cooked take the cucumber out of the fridge and squeeze to remove as much liquid as possible.
15. Mix the cucumber with the garlic, ginger and yoghurt. Add the lemon juice and more salt to taste.

To serve the meal
Serve Lamb Machboos with the cucumber yoghurt and pita bread.

Simple Lamb Stew - *serves 4*

 An excellent hearty favourite that is always well received. You can vary this to suit your taste with beef. Try adding some mixed herbs, either dried or fresh, or try making the beef version and substituting the cup of water for a cup of Red Wine. If you enjoy spice try adding two table spoons of Thai Red Curry Paste.

Ingredients

- 1kg of lamb, cubed into 2.5cm pieces
- 2 tbsp plain flour lightly seasoned with salt and pepper
- 1 tbsp olive oil
- 2 large onions, cut into quarters
- 2 cloves of garlic, crushed
- 1 stalk of celery, sliced into 2 cm lengths
- 1 parsnip, cubed into 1.5 cm cubes
- 1 carrot, cubed into 1.5 cm cubes
- 2 potatoes, cut into quarters
- 2 tbsp soy sauce
- 3 cups of water
- ½ cup of barley
- 1 vegetable stock cube
- 1 packet of dried green peas
- salt and pepper to taste

Method

1. Toss the cubed meat in seasoned flour.
2. Heat the oil in the inner pot.
3. Add the onions and garlic and cook over a medium heat until they are transparent.
4. Remove the inner pot from the heat.
5. Add the vegetables, soy sauce and water to the inner pot with the cooked onions and garlic.
6. Bring the contents to the boil over a medium heat and add the meat, barley, stock and dried peas.
7. Bring back to the boil and boil for 3 to 4 minutes.
8. Put on the lid, turn off the heat and transfer the inner pot into the vacuum-insulated outer container.
9. Close the lid and leave to cook for a minimum of 3 hours. If you leave it longer it will not matter.

Lamb Shanks on Couscous - serves 4

 Serving lamb shanks on couscous is a new way to present an old favourite.

Ingredients

- 4 lamb shanks, trimmed to fit the pot
- ½ cup of flour lightly seasoned with salt and pepper
- 4 large onions, cut into quarters
- 3 cloves of garlic, crushed
- 3 potatoes, cut into large chunks
- 4 carrots, sliced thickly
- 4 large chunks of pumpkin
- ½ tbsp mixed dried herbs
- A small bunch of parsley, finely chopped
- 2 tbsp curry powder (mild, medium or hot as required) made into a paste with a little water
- 2 tbsp tomato paste
- 3 cups of beef stock or 1 cup of white wine and 2 cups of stock
- 1 cup of chick peas, soaked over night
- salt and pepper to taste
- 400g couscous

Method

1. Toss the shanks in seasoned flour.
2. Place the shanks, onions, garlic, vegetables and herbs into the inner pot.
3. Mix together the curry paste, tomato paste and stock. Add to the mixture. Top up with water if the shanks are not covered.
4. Add the pre-soaked chick peas.
5. Bring to the boil and boil for 3 to 4 minutes.
6. Put on the lid, turn off the heat and transfer the inner pot into the vacuum-insulated outer container.
7. Close the lid and leave to cook for a minimum of 6 hours*. If you leave it longer it will not matter.
8. Cook the couscous separately to the packet instructions when you are ready to eat.

* If you like your shanks really falling off the bone after 6 hours bring back to the boil and give them another 6 hours before serving them.

To serve the meal
Serve the couscous as an accompaniment to the main meal.

Lancashire Hot Pot - *serves 4 to 6*

Some people say that female mill workers would prepare this dish in the morning and place it in the range for the family's evening meal. Others say that mine workers would take it to the mines for lunch, wrapped in blankets to keep it hot. Whatever story is true, it's certainly a great meal to cook in a thermal cooker.

Ingredients

- 1kg of lamb or mutton deboned neck, cut into 4 cm cubes
- 2 tbsp seasoned flour for dusting
- groundnut oil
- 3 medium onions, sliced
- 2 sprigs of thyme
- 50g of unsalted butter
- 1 litre of lamb stock (if using stock cubes use two in 1 litre of boiling water).
- ½ tsp of Worcestershire sauce.
- 900g of potatoes, cut into 1 cm thick slices.
- Salt and pepper to taste

Method

1. Dry the lamb with kitchen paper before dusting with 1 tablespoon of the seasoned flour.
2. Add 2 tablespoons of oil to the inner pot and fry the lamb in batches until it is browned all over. Remove each batch as it is browned.
3. Add 2 more tablespoons of oil to the inner pot.
4. Add the onions and thyme. Cook until the onions start to colour.
5. Add the butter and cook for a few more minutes.
6. Sprinkle in the remaining seasoned flour and mix with the onions.
7. Slowly add the stock, stirring all the time to avoid any lumps.
8. Bring to the boil, add the Worcester sauce and check the seasoning. Adjust by adding salt and pepper if necessary.
9. Simmer for 5 minutes and then remove the onions in stock into another container to add later.
10. Now start to assemble the hotpot by placing a layer of potatoes overlapping in the bottom of the inner pot.
11. Next put a layer of lamb followed by a layer of onions and the sauce they were cooked in.
12. Now put another layer of potatoes and continue layering potatoes, lamb and onions until everything is used up. End on a layer of potatoes.
13. Put the thermal cooker inner pot on the stove and bring the contents to the boil and boil for 3 to 4 minutes.
14. Put on the lid, turn off the heat and transfer the inner pot into the vacuum-insulated outer container.
15. Close the lid and leave to cook for a minimum of 3 hours. If you leave it longer it will not matter.

Rosemary Lamb Stew - serves 4

 Rosemary and lamb are a marriage made in heaven.

Ingredients

- 1kg lean lamb, cut into 2.5cm cubes
- 400g tin of diced tomatoes, don't drain
- 300g small potatoes
- 4 carrots, sliced into chunks
- 1 onion, finely diced
- 1 capsicum, finely diced
- 1 sprig fresh rosemary
- 1 lamb stock cube
- water to cover
- salt and freshly ground black pepper
- water

Method

1. Put all the ingredients into the inner pot with enough water to just cover the contents.
2. Bring to the boil and boil for 3 to 4 minutes.
3. Put on the lid, turn off the heat and transfer the inner pot into the vacuum-insulated outer container.
4. Close the lid and leave to cook for a minimum of 3 hours. If you leave it longer it will not matter.
5. Before serving, check the seasoning and add salt and pepper if needed.

Cawl  - serves 4 to 6

 Cawl is considered the national dish of Wales. There are a large number of regional variations. It usually contains meat, normally cut into small pieces, and this may be lamb or mutton beef, pork or bacon, the bacon sometimes being added as an accompaniment to another meat.

Ingredients

- 1 neck of lamb, cut into chunks
- 1 smoked ham hock, soaked overnight in water and rinsed
- 1 large onion, roughly chopped
- 3 leeks - 2 chopped into 2cm lengths. 1 finely chopped for garnish
- 1 small parsnip, cut into 2 cm pieces
- 500g of small potatoes
- 1 small swede, cut into 2 cm cubes
- 12 black peppercorns.
- 2 bay leaves
- 4 sprigs of thyme
- 2 cloves of garlic, sliced
- water
- salt & pepper to taste

Method

1. Put all the ingredients into the inner pot with the ham hock on top.
2. Put in enough water to cover the ingredients.
3. Bring the pot to the boil, skimming off any scum that forms.
4. Boil for 3 to 4 minutes.
5. Put on the lid, turn off the heat and transfer the inner pot into the vacuum-insulated outer container.
6. Close the lid and leave to cook for a minimum of 4 hours. If you leave it longer it will not matter.
7. Before serving, remove the ham hock and take the meat off the bone and put back into the pot.

To serve the meal
Serve, garnished with finely chopped leeks on top.

The fat on the lamb: You can either trim the fat before cooking, or the fat can be skimmed off the broth during cooking.

Spiced Lamb Stew - serves 4

 Just adjust the amount of chilli in this dish to suit your taste.

Ingredients

- 4 small lamb shanks
- Salt and freshly ground black pepper
- ½ tsp chilli powder
- 2 tbsp flour
- 2 tbsp olive oil
- 2 red onions, finely chopped
- 3 cloves garlic, crushed
- 1 chilli chopped or 1/2 tsp chilli powder
- 2 tbsp rosemary leaves
- 2 sticks celery, sliced
- 2 carrots, finely chopped
- 2 tbsp balsamic vinegar
- 1 cup red wine
- 400g tin of chopped tomatoes
- 1 cup beef stock
- ½ cup barley
- mashed potato
- small bunch fresh parsley, chopped.

Method

1. Season flour with salt, pepper and chilli powder then toss lamb in the flour.
2. In the inner pot, over medium heat, brown lamb in 1 tablespoon of oil.
3. Once browned, remove and put to one side.
4. Add the remaining oil to the pot.
5. Add the onions, garlic, chilli, rosemary, celery and carrots. Cook until the onions are soft.
6. Deglaze the pot by adding the balsamic vinegar and wine. Stir to loosen any brown bits caught on the bottom.
7. Increase heat and boil until reduced by half.
8. Reduce heat and stir in tomatoes, stock, barley, and the browned lamb shanks.
9. Return to the boil and boil for 3 to 4 minutes.
10. Put on the lid, turn off the heat and transfer the inner pot into the vacuum-insulated outer container.
11. Close the lid and leave to cook for a minimum of 4 to 5 hours. If you leave it longer it will not matter.

To serve the meal
Serve with mashed potato and sprinkle with parsley.

Lamb Biryani - serves 4 to 6

This Indian biryani, adapted for the Shuttle Chef, can be served on its own as a scrumptious meal, or dressed up for a festive occasion with fresh tomato chutney, vegetable curry side-dishes and crunchy popadoms.

Ingredients

- 1kg lamb or mutton, cut into 2 cm cubes.

For the Marinade
- 4 green chillies, seeded and finely chopped
- Coriander leaves, chopped - about 1 cup full
- 1 clove garlic, crushed with salt
- 2 tsp cumin powder
- 1 tsp chilli powder
- 1 tsp garam masala
- 1 small carton plain yoghurt (approximately 2 large serving spoons)

For the main recipe
- 4 medium onions, thinly sliced
- 1 tbsp oil or ghee
- 0.5kg potatoes (can be either old potatoes peeled and cut into large chunks, or new potatoes halved)
- pinch of saffron (optional, but adds a subtle flavour)
- 3 cups of long grain Basmati or Patna rice

For garnish
- 100g cashew nuts (or shredded almonds)
- 125g sultanas
- ½ browned onions (prepared earlier)

Method

1. Cut the lamb (mutton) into 2 cm cubes.
2. Chop the chillies finely, crush the garlic, chop the coriander leaves and mix with the marinade spices and yogurt.
3. Coat the meat with the marinade. Cover and put in the fridge for 3 hours or longer.
4. Chop the onions, then fry in ghee or oil until golden with some browning (they should taste sweet). Remove from pan.
5. Add a little ghee or oil to the inner pot and heat marinaded lamb to seal the meat. (I prefer to add the meat a third at a time so that it is easier to turn.)
6. When the lamb is simmering hot, add the potatoes and ½ the fried onions. Stir well and bring back to simmer.
7. Mix the rice with 5 cups of boiling water and 2 teaspoons of salt.
8. Put the saffron in ½ cup hot water.
9. Stir ½ the rice into the lamb and potatoes, then spoon the other ½ of the rice and water on top.
10. Sprinkle the saffron water onto the top of the rice.
11. Make sure it is all simmering hot, put the lid on.
12. Turn off the heat and transfer the inner pot into the vacuum-insulated outer container.
13. Close the lid and leave to cook for a minimum of 3 hours. If you leave it longer it will not matter.

To serve the meal

Heat the remaining ½ of the browned onions, then add the nuts and sultanas. Stir occasionally until heated (the sultanas will become plump). Open the thermal cooker and stir the onion, nuts and sultana garnish into the top layer of rice. Serve with fresh tomato chutney (recipe on page 105).

Greek Lamb Stew - serves 4

 A stew with the sunny flavours of Greece.

Ingredients

- 2 tbsp olive oil
- 700g lamb fillet, cut into chunks
- 2 onions, chopped
- 1 red chilli, split lengthways leaving top intact but with seeds removed
- 2 cloves of garlic, crushed
- 1 sprig of rosemary
- 275ml white wine
- 400g tin chopped tomatoes
- 45ml sliced black olives
- 100g linguine, broken into small pieces
- 150g feta cheese
- 15g fresh mint, chopped

Method

1. In the inner pot, over medium heat, brown lamb in 1 tbsp oil.
2. Once browned remove and put to one side.
3. Add the remaining oil to the pot.
4. Add the onions. Cook until the onions are soft.
5. Add the chilli, garlic, rosemary, wine, tomatoes and the lamb.
6. Bring to the boil and boil for 3 to 4 minutes.
7. Put on the lid, turn off the heat and transfer the inner pot into the vacuum-insulated outer container.
8. Close the lid and leave to cook for a minimum of 2 hours.
9. 30 minuets before serving, remove the inner pot add the olives and linguine.
10. Bring to the boil. Put the lid on and place it back into the vacuum-insulated outer container.
11. Leave for 30 minutes.
12. Just before serving, remove the rosemary and chilli.

To serve the meal
Add the feta cheese and mint and serve with a fresh green salad.

Moroccan Pumpkin & Lamb - serves 4 to 6

 Shut your eyes while eating this and image you are on holiday in Morocco.

Ingredients

- 3 tbsp olive oil
- 1 large onion, chopped
- 3 cloves garlic, crushed
- 500g lean lamb, cubed
- 2 large carrots, sliced
- 1 tsp ground turmeric
- ½ tsp hot chilli powder
- 1 cinnamon stick
- 600ml vegetable stock
- 750g pumpkin, cut into chunks
- 400g tin chickpeas, rinsed and drained
- Small handful coriander leaves, chopped
- salt and pepper to taste
- 400g couscous (to serve)

Method

1. Heat up the oil in the inner pot.
2. Sauté the onions and garlic in the oil over medium heat until onions are soft.
3. Add the lamb, carrots and spices. Stir-fry about 3 minutes.
4. Reduce heat and add stock. Bring slowly to the boil.
5. Add pumpkin and chickpeas and bring back to the boil and boil for 3 to 4 minutes.
6. Put on the lid, turn off the heat and transfer the inner pot into the vacuum-insulated outer container.
7. Close the lid and leave to cook for a minimum of 3 hours. If you leave it longer it will not matter.
8. Remove cinnamon stick, add salt and pepper to taste and stir in coriander.

To serve the meal

Serve with couscous made according to the instructions on the packet.

 *Mains Beef*

Beef is used in traditional dishes throughout the world. Some cuts are not used often because they need long, slow cooking. By using the thermal cooker you can save money and make delicious beef dishes with these cuts.

Chilli Con Carne - serves 4 to 6

 Chilli con carne, the official dish of the USA state of Texas, is a great meal for a party. Why not let everyone serve themselves from the thermal cooker.

Ingredients

- 2 tbsp of olive oil
- 50g chorizo, cut into small cubes
- 450g beef, cut into cubes
- 1 onion, minced
- 2 cloves of garlic, minced
- 150ml beef stock
- 150ml of beer
- 1½ tsp of chilli powder
- 400g tin of chopped tomatoes
- 2 tsp of oregano
- 2 tsp of cumin seeds, toasted and ground
- 2 tbsp of tomato paste
- 410g tin of red kidney beans
- ½ a lemon, cut into small pieces
- 1 tsp of salt
- 2 tbsp of cornflower, made into a smooth paste with a little water
- 1 cup of basmati rice
- 2 cups of water
- 2 tsp of salt

Method

1. Put the oil in the inner pot and bring up to medium heat.
2. Add the chorizo and fry to release the oil.
3. Add the beef and cook until it has browned all over.
4. Put in the minced onions and garlic and cook for about 5 minutes.
5. Pour in the beer and beef stock. Add the chilli powder, chopped tomatoes, tomato paste and oregano.
6. Bring to the boil, then turn down to a simmer.
7. Add the ground cumin, drained kidney beans, the lemon pieces and the salt.
8. Take the pot off the heat and slowly add the cornflower mixture, stirring all the time.
9. Put back on heat for 3 minutes.
10. Turn off the heat and transfer the inner pot into the vacuum insulated outer container.
11. Close the lid and leave to cook for a minimum of 3 hours. If you leave it longer it will not matter.

To serve the meal

Check seasoning and add salt if required before serving on a bed of fragrant steamed rice which you can cook in a Mr D's Top Pot (see page 103) if you have one.

Idea: Add a little grated dark chocolate to this dish to give it a great depth of flavour.

Pasta Bake - *serves 4*

 There is no need to precook the pasta in this dish.

Ingredients

- 500g of beef meat balls (or make your own...see recipe below)
- 2 tbsp oil
- 2 onions, coarsely chopped
- 2 cloves of garlic, crushed
- 1 stick of celery, sliced
- 1 cup of sliced mushrooms
- 750ml jar of tomato pasta sauce
- 750ml of water
- salt and pepper to taste
- good pinch of mixed herbs
- ½ cup of chopped fresh parsley
- 1½ cups of penne pasta
- grated cheese to serve

Method

1. Heat 1 tablespoon of oil in the inner pot over a low medium heat.
2. Brown the meat balls in two lots and place to one side.
3. Add onions, garlic and celery. Cook until the onions start to turn clear and soften.
4. Add the mushrooms and stir fry a further minute.
5. Add the meat balls back into the pot and stir in the pasta sauce and water.
6. Add seasoning and herbs herbs.
7. Bring the mixture to the boil.
8. Add the pasta, bring back to the boil.
9. Put on the lid, turn off the heat and put the inner pot into the vacuum-insulated outer container.
10. Close the lid and leave to cook for a minimum of 1 hour. If you leave it longer it will not matter.

To serve the meal
Serve with grated cheese and tossed green salad of your choice.

Make Your Own Meat balls
- 400g minced steak
- 1 clove of garlic
- 1 egg
- 1 tbsp plain flour
- salt and pepper to taste

Method
1. Mix all of the ingredients together.
2. Roll into balls approximately 2 cm in diameter.

Boiled Salt Beef & Dumplings - serves 4

Immortalised by the old music hall song, this is a truly traditional Cockney dish. It is still a favourite in London Pubs. The length of time the meat is soaked depends on how salty it is; check with the butcher. The greyish colour turns an appetising pink when cooked.

Ingredients

- 1kg salted silverside or brisket, soaked overnight in cold water
- 10 black peppercorns
- a few sprigs of thyme
- 2 cloves
- 2 blades of mace
- 2 bay leaf
- 4 small onions, peeled
- 12 small carrots, trimmed and scraped
- 2 small turnips, peeled and quartered
- 2 celery sticks, chopped
- 1 leek, chopped and washed

For the horseradish dumplings

- 125g plain flour, sieved
- 1 tsp baking powder
- 1 tsp salt
- 65g shredded beef suet
- 1 tbsp horseradish sauce
- water

Method

1. Make the dumplings by placing the baking powder, the suet in a clean bowl and add the flour.
2. Mix the flour and suet together.
3. Season with salt and pepper then mix in the horseradish.
4. Make a well in the centre and add the water a bit at a time, mixing until you get a firm dough.
5. Turn the dough out onto a floured surface and roll it into a sausage shape about 4 to 5cms in diameter.
6. Cut off pieces of the dough and shape them into 8 golf ball sized dumplings. They should double in size when cooked. Put to one side.
7. Drain the beef and rinse in cold water, then put in the inner pot of the thermal cooker with peppercorns, thyme, cloves, mace and bay leaves.
8. Cover with water to about 5cm above the beef and bring to the boil.
9. Skim and simmer gently for 5 minutes.
10. Add the vegetables. (You may then need to remove a little of water).
11. Add the dumplings on the top.
12. Bring the pot back to the boil and boil for 3 to 4 minutes.
13. Put on the lid, turn off the heat and transfer the inner pot into the vacuum-insulated outer container.
14. Close the lid and leave to cook for a minimum of 4 hours. If you leave it longer it will not matter.

To serve the meal
To serve, remove the meat and cut into hearty slices. Put two slices on a plate with a selection of the vegetables and dumplings. Pour over some of the stock and serve.

Spiced Beef - *serves minimum 6*

 Sometimes referred to as 'huntsman's beef' and at one time a popular dish all over Britain. The longer the beef is cured, the longer it will keep.

Cooked Spiced Beef will keep for 3-4 weeks in a fridge. Make sure it is well wrapped in foil to prevent it drying out..

Ingredients

- **1.5kg piece of boned and rolled brisket, topside, or thick flank**
- **80g sea salt**
- **10g saltpetre**
- **15g coarsely ground black peppercorns**
- **15g ground all spice**
- **15g ground juniper berries**
- **50g dark brown sugar, such as muscovado**

NOTE: Saltpetre is used in commercial charcuterie and meat curing . If it's difficult to get hold of in small quantities, try the Natural Casing Company in Farnham, Surrey (01252 713545 www.naturalcasingco.co.uk).

Method

1. Mix all the ingredients together and rub well into the beef. Cover and leave in the fridge for 10-12 days, turning it once or twice a day.
2. After 10 to 12 days, wipe off the bits of marinade from the meat, put into a boil in the bag* and seal the bag with a tie.
3. Put the bag containing the meat into the inner pot of the thermal cooker.
4. Fill the pot with water up to about 3cms from the top.
5. Put the pot on the heat and bring to the boil. and boil for 4 to 5 minutes.
6. Put on the lid, turn off the heat and transfer the inner pot into the vacuum-insulated outer container.
7. Close the lid and leave to cook for 4 to 7 hours.
8. Once cooked, remove the bag containing the meat from the pot and leave to cool. This will take about 3 hours.
9. Remove the beef from the bag. Wrap the beef in cling film. Put it in a dish and cover with a weighted plate.
10. Refrigerate for 24 hours.
11. Re-wrap, and keep in the fridge and use for up to 3 weeks.

To serve the meal
Serve cold thinly sliced.

* Only use bags that are designed for boil in the bag cooking. Other plastic food bags must not be used. Contact mail@MrDsKitchen.co.uk if you have problems.

Beef in Mushroom Sauce - serves 4

 Choose a good cream of mushroom soup for this recipe as it forms the base for this quick-to-produce meal.

Ingredients

- 2 tbsp vegetable oil
- 500g minced beef
- ½ cup onion, finely chopped
- 2 cloves garlic, crushed
- 2 cups frozen mixed vegetables, thawed and drained
- 1 tin cream of mushroom soup
- ½ cup milk
- 220g mushrooms
- 2 tsp French mustard
- 1 tsp dried mixed herbs
- salt and pepper to taste
- ½ cup grated cheese for serving

Method

1. Heat the oil in the inner pot.
2. Add the onions and garlic. Sauté them over medium heat.
3. Add the beef and stir-fry until meat browns.
4. Reduce heat.
5. Stir in mixed vegetables until well mixed, then add all other ingredients except for cheese.
6. Bring to the boil and boil for 3 to 4 minutes.
7. Put on the lid, turn off the heat and transfer the inner pot into the vacuum-insulated outer container.
8. Close the lid and leave to cook for a minimum of 1 hour. If you leave it longer it will not matter.

To serve the meal
Serve with grated cheese.

Mains Pork

Pork is one of the most versatile meats to use with your thermal cooker. Fresh meat can be pot roasted and stewed, while processed products, like sausage and bacon, work great in soups, casseroles, and bean dishes. Virtually all cuts of pork can be thermal cooked.

Andrew's Spare Ribs - serves 2 to 4

 These are named after the chef who taught me how to cook this dish.

Ingredients

- 1kg of pork spare ribs (try to purchase ones trimmed of most of the fat). Make sure also the membrane is removed
- 1 red onion, chopped
- 500ml bottle tomato ketchup
- 3 cups of water
- 1 Maggi stock cube
- 2 tbsp Lea & Perrins Worcester Sauce
- 1 cup of Sprite *
- ½ tsp salt

* Sprite is used as a tenderiser.

Method

1. Put all the ingredients into your thermal cooker inner pot.
2. Bring to the boil.
3. Skim off any impurities that form on the surface and boil for 3 to 4 minutes.
4. Put on the lid, turn off the heat and transfer the inner pot into the vacuum-insulated outer container.
5. Close the lid and leave to cook for a minimum of 3 hours. If you leave it longer it will not matter.

Pork Meatball Carbonara - *serves 4*

 There is no need to precook the pasta in this dish.

Ingredients

Meat Balls
- 400g of pork mince
- 2 cloves of garlic
- 1 large egg
- 1 tbsp parsley, finely chopped
- 1 tbsp plain flour
- pinch of salt and pepper

Sauce
- 2 tbsp olive oil
- 2 onions, coarsely chopped
- 1 crushed clove of garlic
- 1 stick of celery, sliced
- 2 courgettes, sliced
- 1 x 500ml jar of carbonara sauce
- 500ml of chicken stock
- ½ a cup of fresh parsley, chopped
- salt and pepper to taste
- 1½ cups of spiral pasta
- grated cheese to serve

Method

1. Mix together the pork mince, garlic, egg, finely chopped parsley, flour, salt and pepper.
2. Separate into small portions.
3. Roll these portions into 2cm balls.
4. Heat 1 tablespoon of oil in the inner pot over a medium heat.
5. Brown the meat balls in two lots and place them to one side.
6. Add one further tablespoon of oil to the saucepan and brown the onions over a low heat for 2-3 minutes.
7. Add the garlic and celery and continue to cook for a few minutes until the onions start to clear and soften.
8. Add the courgettes and stir-fry for a further minute.
9. Add the meat balls back into the inner pot and stir in the parsley.
10. Add the carbonara sauce and the stock.
11. Bring the mixture to the boil.
12. Add the pasta to the sauce and bring back to the boil.
13. Put on the lid, turn off the heat and transfer the inner pot into the vacuum-insulated outer container.
14. Close the lid and leave to cook for a minimum of 2 hours. If you leave it longer it will not matter.

To serve the meal
Serve with grated cheese and a tossed green salad of your choice.

BBQ Red Wine Rib Rack - serves 2 to 4

 This is a really quick and easy recipe that turns out delicious BBQ ribs with a smoky red wine flavour. You can serve these on a bed of mashed potato, or rice (if you are using the two pot system these can be cooked while you are cooking the ribs) or with garden salad and fresh crusty bread.

Ingredients

- 1kg of pork spare ribs (try to purchase ones trimmed of most of the fat). Make sure also the membrane is removed
- 3 medium onions, thinly sliced
- 1 tbsp olive oil
- 4 shallots, thinly sliced
- 2 containers of smoky **BBQ** marinade (Stubbs is good)
- 1 cup of red wine (use more or less to suit your taste)
- 1 cup of water
- parsley for garnish

Method

1. Marinade the rib racks with the BBQ marinade and put in the fridge for at least 2 hours. Overnight would be better.
2. Put the oil into the inner pot and place it on the stove top over a medium heat.
3. Add the sliced onions and shallots and stir fry until the onions become soft.
4. Take this off the heat and add all the remaining BBQ marinade and water with the red wine of your choice (and quantity).
5. Put the saucepan back on the stove.
6. Place the rib racks into the sauce.
7. Bring to the boil and boil for 3 to 4 minutes.
8. Put on the lid, turn off the heat and transfer the inner pot into the vacuum-insulated outer container.
9. Close the lid and leave to cook for a minimum of 4 to 5 hours. If you leave it longer it will not matter.

To serve the meal
1. Remove the rib racks and place to one side
2. Return the inner saucepan to the stove top and bring all the liquid to the boil.
3. Vigorously boil this liquid, stirring regularly, until it is reduced by half and is nice and thick.
4. Place the rib racks onto a suitable plate.
5. Pour the thickened sauce over the top of the racks.
6. Garnish with fresh parsley.

Pork in Master Stock - *serves 4*

 This dish is very good cold or can be shredded and served with rice and stir fry vegetables.

Ingredients

- **The master Stock from page 98**
- **1.5kg Pork joint**

Method

1. Wash the pork well.
2. Place the pork in the inner pot of the thermal cooker.
3. Pour over the master stock, making sure the pork is covered.
4. Bring to the boil and boil for 4 or 5 minutes.
5. Put on the lid, turn off the heat and transfer the inner pot into the vacuum-insulated outer container.
6. Close the lid and leave to cook for a minimum of 4 hours. If you leave it longer it will not matter.

Pork Chops in Cider - serves 4

 Use vintage cider for this recipe to get that great apple flavour that goes so well with pork.

Ingredients

- **4 pork chops**
- **50g butter**
- **2 tbsp olive oil**
- **1 large onion, sliced**
- **175g mushrooms, sliced**
- **2 tbsp plain flour**
- **500ml vintage cider**
- **6 tbsp double cream**
- **Salt and pepper to taste**

Method

1. Melt the butter and olive oil in the inner pot and brown the chops in two batches.
2. Once browned put to one side.
3. Add the onion and mushrooms and cook until the onion is soft. Don't let it brown.
4. Add the flour and stir to coat the onion and mushrooms.
5. Slowly pour in the cider, stirring to avoid lumps. This shouldn't happen if you have mixed the flour well with the onion mushroom mix.
6. Once you have a smooth sauce, pour in the cream and mix well.
7. Put the chops back in the pot and make sure that they are covered with the sauce.
8. Bring to the boil and boil for 3 to 4 minutes.
9. Put on the lid, turn off the heat and transfer the inner pot into the vacuum-insulated outer container.
10. Close the lid and leave to cook for a minimum of 2 hours. If you leave it longer it will not matter.

To serve the meal
Serve with potatoes and fresh vegetables.

Cooking vegetables at the same time
By using the lidded top pot (available from Mr D's cookware) you can cook your vegetables at the same time.

Pot Roast Pork - serves 4 to 6

 This is a great way to cook pork. It keeps it moist, good for eating hot and in a sandwich the following day.

Ingredients

- olive oil
- **700g leg of pork, boned and tied with string to stop it falling apart**
- **½ bunch spring onions, thinly sliced**
- **2 cm piece ginger, thinly sliced**
- **Pepper**
- **500ml water**
- **500ml chicken stock**
- **375ml soy sauce**
- **375ml white wine**
- **125g sugar**
- **Pepper**

Method

1. Heat 1 tablespoon of olive oil in the inner pot.
2. Add the pork, onions and ginger.
3. Brown the pork all over.
4. Add the water, chicken stock, soy sauce, wine, sugar and some freshly ground pepper to taste.
5. Bring to the boil and boil for 3 to 4 minutes.
6. Put on the lid, turn off the heat and transfer the inner pot into the vacuum-insulated outer container.
7. Close the lid and leave to cook for a minimum of 3 hours. If you leave it longer it will not matter.

To serve the meal

To serve, untie string from pork and slice thickly. Pour a little of the cooking liquid over the slices.

Tip
Remember to save any of the cooking liquid you have left to use as stock in other dishes.

Pork Sausage Casserole - serves 4

 Sausages, potatoes and carrots are the ideal ingredients for a one pot meal.

Ingredients

- 2 tbsp olive oil
- 8 pork sausages, pricked to help stop them from splitting
- 1 red onion, cut into wedges
- 1 clove of garlic, finely chopped
- 1 tsp paprika
- 500g small potatoes
- 4 carrots, sliced
- 400g tin of chopped tomatoes
- 400ml vegetable stock
- Small bunch of sage leaves, chopped
- salt & pepper to taste

Method

1. Heat the olive oil in the inner pot.
2. Add the sausages and cook them over a medium heat until they are browned.
3. Remove the sausages. Turn down the heat and add the garlic and paprika. Cook for 1 minute. Make sure it doesn't burn or it will go bitter.
4. Add the onion chunks and cook until soft.
5. Stir in the potatoes and carrots so that they are covered with oil.
6. Put the sausages back in the pot.
7. Add the tomatoes, vegetable stock and the sage.
8. Bring to the boil and boil for 3 to 4 minutes.
9. Put on the lid, turn off the heat and transfer the inner pot into the vacuum-insulated outer container.
10. Close the lid and leave to cook for a minimum of 2 hours. If you leave it longer it will not matter.
11. Before serving, check the seasoning and adjust if needed.

Chinese Pork & Vegetables - serves 4 to 6

 The taste of China produced in a thermal cooker.

Ingredients

- 400g diced pork
- 2 cm piece ginger
- 4 water chestnuts
- 8 dried shitake mushrooms
- 12 snow peas

Stock

- 1 cup water
- ½ cup white wine
- 1½ tbsp sugar
- 2½ tbsp rice vinegar
- 3 tbsp soy sauce

Method

1. Soak the mushrooms in water and put to one side.
2. Place pork in inner pot with finely sliced ginger and stock ingredients.
3. Bring to the boil and boil for 3 to 4 minutes.
4. Put on the lid, turn off the heat and transfer the inner pot into the vacuum-insulated outer container.
5. Close the lid and leave to cook for a minimum of 2 hours. If you leave it longer it will not matter.
6. Before serving remove the inner pot from outer pot and place back on low heat.
7. Add soaked mushrooms, snow peas and water chestnuts and simmer for 5 minutes.

To serve the meal
serve with rice.

To Thermal Cook Rice
See page 103 for the method of cooking rice with the lidded top pot.

Pork Tenderloin - *serves 4*

 Try a different soup mix and make your own variation to this easy recipe.

Ingredients

- 1kg pork tenderloin
- 1 packet dry onion soup mix
- 235 ml water
- 180 ml red wine
- 25g minced garlic
- 45 ml soy sauce
- freshly ground black pepper to taste

Method

1. Place pork tenderloin in the inner pot.
2. Add the contents of the soup packet.
3. Pour over the water, wine, and soy sauce.
4. Turn the pork in the liquid to make sure that it is coated.
5. Carefully spread garlic over the pork, leaving as much on top of the roast during cooking as possible.
6. Sprinkle with pepper and bring to the boil.
7. Once boiling boil for 3 to 4 minutes.
8. Put on the lid, turn off the heat and transfer the inner pot into the vacuum-insulated outer container.
9. Close the lid and leave to cook for a minimum of 4 hours. If you leave it longer it will not matter.
10. Before serving, check the seasoning and adjust if needed.

To serve the meal
Serve with cooking liquid as a gravy.

Paprika Pork Casserole - *serves 4*

 After a busy day this casserole is the ideal meal when you return home.

Ingredients

- 100g pork fillet, sliced
- 25g plain flour
- Salt & pepper
- 15ml paprika
- 50g of butter
- 1 onion, chopped
- 250ml stock
- 60ml sherry
- 250g mushrooms, sliced
- 150ml soured cream

Method

1. Season the flour with salt and pepper and paprika.
2. Coat the pork with the seasoned flour.
3. Heat the butter in the inner pot.
4. Add the pork and fry until coloured.
5. Add the onion, stock, sherry and mushrooms and stir thoroughly.
6. Bring to the boil and boil for 3 to 4 minutes.
7. Put on the lid, turn off the heat and transfer the inner pot into the vacuum-insulated outer container.
8. Close the lid and leave to cook for a minimum of 2 hours. If you leave it longer it will not matter.

To serve the meal

Before serving stir in the soured cream and check seasoning. This dish is good served with noodles.

Beans & Sausages - serves 4 to 6

 When you are looking for comfort food you can't beat beans & sausages. Make sure they are good quality sausages.

Ingredients

- 2 tbsp olive oil
- 8 pork sausages
- 125g smoked bacon lardons
- 1 clove of garlic, crushed
- 1 red onion, sliced
- 500g small potatoes
- 500ml of chicken or vegetable stock
- 2 cans of butter beans, drained
- salt & pepper to taste

Method

1. Add the olive oil to the inner pot.
2. Fry the sausages until they are browned.
3. Remove them and put to one side.
4. Add the bacon lardons, onions and garlic. Cook until the onions are softened.
5. Cut the sausages in two and add them to the pot, along with the butter beans and potatoes.
6. Pour in the stock. It should just cover the contents, but if not add a little water.
7. Bring to the boil and boil for 3 to 4 minutes.
8. Put on the lid, turn off the heat and transfer the inner pot into the vacuum-insulated outer container.
9. Close the lid and leave to cook for a minimum of 2 hours. If you leave it longer it will not matter.

# Mains Vegetarian

Vegetarian food is not just for those who don't eat meat. Grains, beans and pasta are enjoyed by everyone. Vegetables cooked in a thermal cooker will keep their shape and retain their vitamins.

Some of these recipes are suitable for Vegans and others can be adapted.

Mushroom Biryani - serves 4

 This biryani has an amazing depth of flavour and will be a hit with both vegetarians and non vegetarians.

Ingredients

For Mushrooms:
- a large handful of mint
- a large handful of coriander
- a large handful of basil
- 6 tbsp natural yoghurt
- 1 garlic clove
- 2 small green chillies, deseeded
- 25g ghee or vegetable oil
- 200g mixed wild mushrooms

For Rice:
- a pinch of saffron threads
- 3 star anise
- 8 cardamom pods
- 1 tsp fennel seeds
- 2 pieces of mace (optional)
- 1 tsp of turmeric
- 1 tsp of salt
- 2 cups of water
- 1 cup of rice

Note: use soya yoghurt for Vegan biryani.

Method

1. Put the saffron in a cup of hot milk to soak.
2. Put the mint, coriander, basil, yoghurt, garlic and chillies in a blender and blend until they become a smooth paste.
3. Heat the ghee or oil in the thermal cookers inner pot and when hot add the mushrooms and cook for 1 minute, stirring occasionally.
4. Add the paste and continue to cook for 4 minutes on medium heat.
5. Put the star anise, cardamom pods, fennel seeds, mace, turmeric and salt, along with 2 cups of water in a pan and bring to the boil.
6. Add the rice, simmer for 1 minute.
7. Spread the rice, water and the spices from the rice water on top of the mushrooms in the inner pot.
8. Pour over the saffron/milk mixture.
9. Bring the inner pot back to the boil, put the lid on.
10. Turn off the heat and transfer the inner pot into the vacuum-insulated outer container.
11. Close the lid and leave to cook for a minimum of 3 hours. If you leave it longer it will not matter.

To serve the meal
Serve with nan bread or chapatti. You can also serve with a vegetable sir fry.
1. You can put some cashew nuts on the top if you like.

Butternut Squash Risotto - serves 2 to 4

 No need to spend time adding stock gradually with this risotto. In this recipe the stock is added all at the same time.

Ingredients

- 1kg butternut squash, peeled, deseeded and cut into 5 cm pieces
- 3 tbsp of olive oil
- 125g of butter
- 1 onion, finely chopped
- 1 garlic clove, finely chopped
- 300g risotto rice
- 1 litre of hot vegetable stock
- 250ml of white wine
- 150g Parmesan cheese
- salt & pepper

Method

1. Put 2 tablespoons of oil in the inner pot and heat.
2. When the oil is hot, add the squash with 1 teaspoon of salt and fry on medium heat for 10 minutes, stirring occasionally.
3. Remove the squash and put on a plate.
4. Melt 50g of butter and 1 tablespoon of olive oil in the inner pot.
5. Add the onions and garlic. Soften on a gentle heat for 5 minutes, (you only want them soft not browned).
6. Add the rice and stir until it is completely coated with butter and oil.
7. Add the hot stock, wine and squash. Stir, bring back to the boil and boil for 3 to 4 minutes.
8. Put on the lid, turn off the heat and transfer the inner pot into the vacuum-insulated outer container.
9. Close the lid and leave to cook for a minimum of 1 hour. If you leave it longer it will not matter.
10. Once ready, stir in the rest of the butter and season to taste with salt and pepper.

To serve the meal
Plate up with grated Parmesan on top.

Chick Pea & Potato Curry - serves 2

 By doubling the ingredients this becomes the ideal meal for a vegetarian dinner party.

Ingredients

- 225g chick peas, soaked overnight. You can use a 410g tin of chick peas. These will not need soaking.
- 3 tbsp vegetable oil
- 1 onion, finely chopped
- 2 garlic cloves, crushed
- 2 cm root ginger, grated
- 1 tsp salt
- 2 tsp ground coriander
- 1 tsp turmeric
- ½ tsp cayenne pepper
- ½ tsp cumin seed
- ½ tsp mustard seed
- 2 tbsp tomato puree
- 400g tin chopped tomatoes, undrained
- 2 large potatoes, cut into 2cm cubes
- 3 tbsp chopped fresh coriander
- 1 tbsp lemon or lime juice
- 500ml vegetable stock
- 1 red onion, thinly sliced to serve.

Method

Cooking the chick peas (if using dried chickpeas)

1. Drain the chick peas and put them in the inner pot.
2. Cover with freshly heated hot water and bring to the boil and boil for 3 to 4 minutes.
3. Put on the lid, turn off the heat and place the inner pot into the vacuum-insulated outer container.
4. Put on the lid and leave for a minimum of 2 hours.
5. Remove the inner pot, drain the chick peas and keep them to one side.

Method for both dried and tinned chick peas

1. Add the oil to the inner pot and heat.
2. Add the onion, garlic and spices mixed to a paste with the tomato puree. Sauté over medium heat until the onions soften.
3. Reduce the heat and stir while adding the remaining ingredients, including the drained chick peas.
4. Bring to the boil and boil for 3 to 4 minutes.
5. Put on the lid, turn off the heat and transfer the inner pot into the vacuum-insulated outer container.
6. Close the lid and leave to cook for a minimum of 1 hour. If you leave it longer it will not matter.

To serve the meal

To serve, garnish with thinly sliced red onion rings.

Spicy Baked Beans - serves 2 to 3

 Baked beans are a favourite with young and old. They can accompany so many meals.

Ingredients

- 1 tsp olive oil
- 2½ cups onions, chopped
- 2 garlic cloves, crushed
- 2 tbsp ginger, freshly grated
- 1 tsp of cayenne pepper
- 2 cups of carrots, finely chopped
- 2 cups apples peeled and finely chopped

- ¾ cup of tomato paste
- ½ cup of Dijon mustard
- 2 tbsp Worcestershire sauce
- ½ cup of brown sugar (or molasses)
- 2 tbsp balsamic vinegar
- 1 cup of tomato sauce
- 1 cup of water
- ½ cup of raisins
- 1 tsp minced chilli
- 1 bay leaf
- 375g of dried haricot beans (Make sure you soak these overnight). Alternatively you can use 2 410g tins of beans and these will not need soaking.

Note: Vegan Worcestershire sauce is available from some supermarkets.

Method

Cooking the haricot beans (if using dried beans)

1. Drain the haricot beans and put them in the inner pot.
2. Cover with freshly heated hot water, bring to the boil and boil for 3 to 4 minutes.
3. Put on the lid, turn off the heat and place the inner pot into the vacuum-insulated outer container.
4. Put on the lid and leave for a minimum of 2 hours.
5. Remove the inner pot, drain the haricot beans and keep them to one side.

Method for both dried and tinned haricot beans

1. Add the oil and onions and fry over medium heat for 3 minutes.
2. Add the garlic, ginger and cayenne, then cool for just 30 seconds, stirring to release their oils.
3. Stir in the carrots and apples until they are well coated with the spices.
4. Add the rest of the ingredients, stir thoroughly, bring to the boil and boil for 3 to 4 minutes.
5. Put on the lid, turn off the heat and transfer the inner pot into the vacuum-insulated outer container.
6. Close the lid and leave to cook for a minimum of 4 hours. If you leave it longer it will not matter.

Pumpkin & Root Vegetable Stew - serves 4

 This is the ideal meal for a vegetarian dinner party.

Ingredients

- 2 tbsp olive oil
- 1 large onion, diced
- 2 cloves garlic, crushed
- 1 small red chilli, deseeded and finely sliced
- 500g pumpkin, cut into 2.5cm cubes
- 2 celery sticks, thickly sliced
- 3 medium carrots, thickly sliced
- 1 small parsnip, thickly sliced

- 400g tin chopped tomatoes
- 1 tbsp tomato paste
- 1 tbsp paprika
- 250ml vegetable stock
- 1 tsp dried mixed herbs
- 400g tin kidney beans, drained
- salt and pepper to taste
- 3-4 tbsp finely chopped parsley, (for serving)

Method

1. Sauté the onions, garlic and chilli in oil over medium heat until onion is soft.
2. Reduce heat, add pumpkin, celery, carrots and parsnip and stir-fry a for a further minute.
3. Add remaining ingredients and bring to the boil and boil for 3 to 4 minutes.
4. Put on the lid, turn off the heat and transfer the inner pot into the vacuum-insulated outer container.
5. Close the lid and leave to cook for a minimum of 2 hours. If you leave it longer it will not matter.

 # Puddings

All kinds of delicious puddings can be made in a thermal cooker. Unlike puddings made in a conventional oven those made in a thermal cooker will stay moist and will not burn.

Some puddings are made directly in the inner pot and others require a bowl or pan which is placed in boiling water inside the inner pot.

Baked Apples with Raisins - *serves 4 to 6*

 The perfect after-dinner winter warmer that will be enjoyed by young and old alike.

Ingredients

- **5 to 6 apples, cored (Granny Smiths are ideal)**
- **½ cup of raisins**
- **½ cup of sugar**
- **2 tbsp ground cinnamon**
- **1 cup of hot water (or apple cider)**

Method

1. Fill the centre of each apple with raisins.
2. Place the apples upright in the inner pot
3. In a bowl, combine the water, cinnamon and sugar, then pour the mixture over the apples.
4. Bring the pot to the boil on low heat and then simmer for five minutes with the lid on.
5. Turn off the heat and transfer the inner pot into the vacuum-insulated outer container.
6. Close the lid and leave to cook for a minimum of 2 hours. If you leave it longer it will not matter.

To serve the meal
Serve with ice cream, cream or yoghurt.

Rice Pudding - *serves 4*

 Try this classic, simple dessert, and let your thermal cooker do all the work.

Ingredients

- **73g pudding rice**
- **3 tbsp castor sugar**
- **750ml full-fat milk**
- **150ml evaporated milk**
- **25g unsalted butter**
- **1 cinnamon stick**
- **strip of lemon peel**

Method

1. Grease a stainless steel cake/pudding tin* or the top pot* (if cooking it with a main meal).
2. Mix all the ingredients together well.
3. Pour the mixed ingredients into the greased container and put on the lid.

If using a cake/pudding tin

1. Place the mixed ingredients inside the cake/pudding tin, put on the lid and place on a trivet inside the inner pot.
2. Add boiling water to come ¾ the way up cake tin.
3. Bring the inner pot to the boil, cover with the lid and turn the heat down to a simmer.
4. Simmer for 20 minutes with the lid on.
5. Turn off the heat and transfer the inner pot into the vacuum-insulated outer container.
6. Close the outer pot lid and leave to cook for a minimum of 1 hour. If you leave it longer it will not matter.
7. Serve hot or cold.

If using a top pot over a main meal

1. Place the mixed ingredients in the top pot and bring gently to simmer point on the hob, stirring intermittently.
2. Carefully place the top pot into the inner pot above the main meal. (The inner pot rim will support the top pot).
3. Put the lid on the inner pot and simmer the main meal for 3 - 5 minutes. (You might want to give it a stir half way through.)
4. Turn off the heat and transfer the inner pot into the vacuum-insulated outer container.
5. Close the lid and leave to cook for the length of time required for the main meal.
6. Serve hot or cold.

* The Mr D's Top Pot and Mr D's Cake/Pudding Tin is available from our cookware range at www.MrDsCookware.com. See the back of the book for details.

Poached Pears in Spiced Wine - *serves 4*

 You can use this recipe with apples instead of pears. It a superb treatment for Pears or Apples that is very visually appealing.

Ingredients

- **4 cooking apples or pears (peeled and cored)**
- **juice and zest of half a lemon**
- **500ml of red wine**
- **½ cup of castor sugar**
- **1 cinnamon stick or 1 tsp of ground cinnamon**
- **6 cloves**
- **thickened cream or yoghurt for serving**

Method

1. Place all of the ingredients except the apples or pears into the inner pot and bring to the boil over a low heat.
2. Add the apples or pears and bring back to the boil.
3. Turn down the heat and simmer gently for 5 minutes with the lid on.
4. Turn off the heat and transfer the inner pot into the vacuum-insulated outer container.
5. Close the lid and leave to cook for a minimum of 2 hours. If you leave it longer it will not matter.

To serve the meal
Serve with thickened cream or yoghurt.

Bread & Butter Pudding - serves 4

What better to do with that left over loaf of bread than concoct a traditional Bread and Butter Pudding?

Ingredients

- 1 tin of evaporated milk
- 180ml of milk
- 2 large eggs
- 3 tbsp castor sugar
- 5 slices of buttered bread, cubed (with the crusts removed)
- 2 tbsp sultanas
- 2 tbsp Grand Marnier liquor
- nutmeg

NOTE: *You can thinly cover the buttered bread with a jam of your choice before cutting them into small cubes.*

---

* The Mr D's Top Pot and Mr D's Cake/Pudding Tin is available from our cookware range at www.MrDsCookware.com. See the back of the book for details.

Method

1. Sprinkle the sultanas with Grand Marnier and leave for at least 1 hour.
2. Arrange the bread and sultanas in a buttered stainless steel cake/pudding tin* or the top pot* (if cooking it with a main meal).
3. Make the custard by heating the milks in a saucepan until it is hot. Don't allow it to boil or you will make scrambled egg at the next stage.
4. Whisk the eggs and sugar together in a bowl, then slowly add the hot milk, whisking all the time.
5. Pour the custard over the bread and sultanas, sprinkle with nutmeg and put on the lid.

If using a cake/pudding tin
1. Place the cake/pudding tin inside the inner pot on a trivet.
2. Add boiling water to come ¾ the way up cake/pudding tin.
3. Bring the inner pot to the boil, cover with the lid and turn the heat down to a simmer.
4. Simmer for 20 minutes with the lid on.
5. Turn off the heat and transfer the inner pot into the vacuum-insulated outer container.
6. Close the lid and leave to cook for a minimum of 3 hours. If you leave it longer it will not matter.

If using a top pot over a main meal
1. Place the top pot, with the lid on, in the inner pot over the your main meal.
2. Simmer the main meal for 15 minutes. You might want to give it a stir half way through.
3. Turn off the heat and transfer the inner pot into the vacuum-insulated outer container.
4. Close the lid and leave to cook for the length of time required for the main meal.

Christmas Pudding - serves 6

This traditional 1 litre Christmas pudding, prepared and cooked in the thermal cooker, couldn't be easier. No more boiling for hours, checking water levels. With the saving in time and energy you could make Christmas Pudding on a more regular basis.

Ingredients

- 150g raisins, chopped
- 100g sultanas
- 100g currants
- 75g of pitted dates, chopped
- 75g of figs or prunes, chopped
- ¼ of a cup of brandy or whisky

Dry Ingredients
- 125g suet
- ¼ cup of plain flour
- 1 cup of fresh bread crumbs
- a pinch of salt
- 1 tsp mixed spice
- ½ tsp ground ginger
- ¾ cup of dark brown sugar
- 2 eggs, lightly beaten
- ¼ cup of lime marmalade
- ¼ tsp of bicarbonate of soda, dissolved in 1 tbsp of boiling water

Cut two circles of baking paper to fit the pudding bowl or cake tin. (one for the base and one for the top). Grease the bowl or tin and line the base with one circle. Place the second circle to lightly rest on the top of the pudding.

Method

1. Heat the brandy or whisky in a saucepan over a medium heat until hot. Don't let it boil.
2. Remove from the heat, add the dried fruit and stir to combine. Cover and leave to stand at room temperature overnight.
3. Combine the dry ingredients, except for the bicarbonate of soda, in a mixing bowl.
4. Prepare the pudding basin as explained in the hints box below.
5. Add the soaked fruit, eggs and bicarbonate of soda. Mix thoroughly to combine.
6. Spoon into the pudding bowl and place a circle of baking paper on top of the mix.
7. Put on the lid. If you do not have a lid cover with eco-friendly foil and tie with string.
8. Place the pudding bowl inside the inner pot on a trivet.
9. Add enough boiling water to come ¾ the way up the side of the bowl.
6. Bring back to the boil.
7. Turn down the heat and simmer gently for 45 minutes with the lid on. Top up with boiling water if necessary to keep the level ¾ the way up the side of the bowl.
8. Turn off the heat and transfer the inner pot into the vacuum-insulated outer container.
9. Close the lid and leave to cook for a minimum of 8 hours. If you leave it longer it will not matter.
10. Test with a skewer, which should come out clean. If not then return the inner pot to a simmer for another 20 minutes then place back into the outer container for 2 more hours.
11. Allow to cool in the bowl.

Umm Ali - serves 4 to 6

This famous Egyptian pudding has its origins in the reign of the Ottoman Turks. One day while hunting in the Nile delta, the hungry sultan stopped in a small village and the best cook of the village, Umm 'Ali, created this dish. The sultan so enjoyed it he asked for it again next time he visited.

Ingredients

- **125g filo pastry**
- **¾ cup pistachios, shelled, chopped**
- **½ cup pine nuts**
- **½ cup slivered almonds**
- **2 tsp sugar**
- **½ - ¾ cups coconut flakes (depending on taste)**
- **½ cup raisins**
- **15oz can of sweetened condensed milk**
- **3 cups water**
- **½ cup single cream**
- **½ tsp vanilla extract**

* The Mr D's Top Pot and Mr D's Cake/Pudding Tin is available from our cookware range at www.MrDsCookware.com. See the back of the book for details.

Method

1. Take several sheets of filo pastry and leave them out until they are completely dry and brittle.
2. Butter a stainless steel cake/pudding tin* or the top pot* (if cooking it with a main meal).
3. Layer with broken pieces of filo pastry.
4. Sprinkle the nuts, sugar, coconut flakes, and raisins over the pastry.
5. Mix together the condensed milk, water, single cream and vanilla extract.
6. Pour the mixture over everything.
7. Put the lid on the stainless steel cake/pudding tin.

If using a cake/pudding tin
1. Place the cake/pudding tin, on a trivet in the inner pot.
2. Add boiling water to come ¾ the way up cake/pudding tin.
3. Bring the inner pot to the boil, cover with the lid and turn the heat down to a simmer.
4. Simmer for 10 minutes with the lid on.
5. Turn off the heat and transfer the inner pot into the vacuum-insulated outer container.
6. Close the lid and leave to cook for a minimum of 1 hour. If you leave it longer it will not matter.

If using a top pot over a main meal
1. Place the top pot, with the lid on in the inner pot over the your main meal.
2. Simmer the main meal for 15 minutes. You might want to give it a stir half way through.
3. Turn off the heat and transfer the inner pot into the vacuum-insulated outer container.
4. Close the lid and leave to cook for the length of time required for the main meal.

Foundation Pudding or Cake - serves 4 to 6

 There are so many different variations you can create from this basic steamed pudding recipe.

Ingredients

- **100g butter**
- **100g sugar**
- **130g self raising flour**
- **125ml milk**
- **1 large egg**

Method

1. Cream butter and sugar, add egg and mix well.
2. Add the flour. Mix until smooth before mixing in the milk.
3. Grease a stainless steel cake/pudding tin * and fill with the mixture.
4. Cover with round of baking paper and put on the lid.
5. Place the tin inside the inner pot on a trivet.
6. Add enough boiling water to come ¾ the way up the side of the cake/pudding tin.
6. Bring to the boil.
7. Turn down the heat and simmer gently for 30 minutes with the lid on.
8. Turn off the heat and transfer the inner pot into the vacuum-insulated outer container.
9. Close the lid and leave to cook for a minimum of 4 hours. If you leave it longer it will not matter.

* A Mr D's Cake/Pudding Tin is available from our cookware range at www.MrDsCookware.com. See the back of the book for details.

Variations:

Add to the basic mixture one of the following.

- Sultana Pudding: 2 tbsp sultanas
- Jam Pudding: 2 tbsp jam to bottom of basin
- Date Pudding: 125g chopped dates
- Coconut Pudding: 3 tbsp coconut, 2 tbsp milk and 4 drops almond essence.
- Chocolate Pudding: 1 tbsp cocoa and ½ tsp vanilla essence.

 # Cakes

You may find it surprising that you can make cakes in a thermal cooker but they are easy to make and will be some of the most moist cakes you are ever likely to eat. Note: a useful conversion chart can be found on page 111.

Christmas Cake - serves 8 to 10

 This is the traditional Christmas or Festival Cake but prepared and cooked in a Thermal Cooker. It couldn't be easier and the results are always so moist. Such an efficient time and energy saver........you could make these on a regular basis as the effort is far less than the reward.

Ingredients

- 150g raisins, chopped
- 100g sultanas
- 100g currants
- 75g pitted dates, chopped
- 75g figs or prunes, chopped
- 50g glace cherries, chopped
- ½ cup of brandy or whisky
- 125g butter, at room temperature
- 100g dark brown sugar
- 1 tbsp treacle
- 1 tsp finely grated orange rind
- 2 large eggs
- 1 cup plain flour
- ¼ cup self raising flour
- 2½ tsp ground cinnamon
- 1 tsp of nutmeg
- ½ cup slivered almonds, toasted
- whole blanched almonds toasted for decorating.

* A Mr D's Cake/Pudding Tin is available from our cookware range at www.MrDsCookware.com. See the back of the book for details.

Lining the tin: Cut two circles of baking paper to fit a cake tin (one for the base and one for the top) that will fit in your thermal cooker. Grease the tin and line the base with one circle.

Method

1. Heat the brandy or whisky in a saucepan over a medium heat until hot. Don't let it boil.
2. Remove from the heat add the dried fruit and stir to combine. Cover and leave to stand at room temperature overnight.
3. Beat the butter, sugar, treacle and orange rind in a bowl until smooth. Add the eggs, 1 at a time, beating well after each addition.
4. Add the flour and spices and fold to combine. Stir in the fruit mixture and slivered almonds.
5. Spoon into the cake/pudding tin* and smooth the surface.
6. Decorate with toasted whole almonds. Cover with the other baking paper circle. Put the lid onto the cake/pudding tin* and clip down (If using another cake tin without a lid, cover with foil and tie securely with string)
7. Place the cake/pudding tin* inside the inner pot on a trivet.
8. Add enough boiling water to come ¾ the way up the side of the cake/pudding tin.
9. Turn the heat down to low simmer.
8. Simmer gently with the lid on for 30 minutes.
6. Turn off the heat and transfer the inner pot into the vacuum-insulated outer container.
7. Close the lid and leave to cook for a minimum of 6 hours. If you leave it longer it will not matter.
8. Test with a skewer, which should come out clean. If not then return the inner pot to a simmer for another 20 minutes then place back into the outer container for 2 more hours.
9. Allow to cool in the tin.

Lemon Drizzle Cake - serves 8 to 10

 This is a wonderful cake and gets eaten very quickly and is loved by everyone.

Ingredients

- 115g unsalted butter, softened
- 115g caster sugar
- 2 medium eggs, beaten
- 115g self-raising flour
- ¼tsp baking powder
- 18g ground almonds
- juice and finely grated zest of ½ lemon
- 100g summer berries (optional)

Ingredients for the drizzle
- juice and finely grated zest of 1½ lemons
- 90g caster sugar

* A Mr D's Cake/Pudding Tin is available from our cookware range at www.MrDsCookware.com. See the back of the book for details.

Lining the tin: Cut two circles of baking paper to fit a cake tin (one for the base and one for the top) that will fit in your thermal cooker. Grease the tin and line the base with one circle.

Method

1. Prepare the cake/pudding tin as described in the box below.
2. In a large bowl cream the butter and sugar until it becomes pale in colour.
3. Slowly add the eggs bit by bit and continue to beat until well combined.
4. With a wooden spoon gradually fold in the flour, ground almonds and baking powder.
5. Fold in the juice and zest of ½ lemon.
6. Spoon the batter into a cake/pudding tin* and spread it out evenly.
7. Put the lid onto the cake/pudding tin* and clip down (If using another cake tin without a lid, cover with foil and tie securely with string)
8. Place the cake/pudding tin* inside the inner pot on a trivet.
9. Add enough boiling water to come ¾ the way up the side of the cake/pudding tin.
10. Turn down the heat to a low simmer and simmer gently with the lid on for 25 to 30 minutes.
11. Turn off the heat and transfer the inner pot into the vacuum-insulated outer container.
12. Close the lid and leave to cook for a minimum of 6 hours. If you leave it longer it will not matter.
13. Once cooked, allow to cool in the tin for a few minutes.
14. Remove from the pan and place on a wire rack.
15. Warm the sugar with the zest and juice of 1½ lemons in a sauce pan, stirring until the sugar dissolves.
16. Put the cake on a plate and prick it in several places with a wooden skewer.
17. Pour the hot sugar/lemon syrup over the warm cake.
18. When the cake is cool, top it with some summer berries (optional) and serve.

Date & Nut Cake - serves 8 to 10

 An excellent, easy to prepare, favourite for most of the family.

Ingredients

- 1 cup of chopped dates
- 1 tsp bicarbonate of soda
- 180ml of boiling water
- 1 tbsp butter
- ½ a cup of brown sugar
- 1 large egg
- 1 cup of self raising flour
- 1 cup of plain flour
- 1 tsp vanilla essence
- ½ a cup of chopped pecans or walnuts

* A Mr D's Cake/Pudding Tin is available from our cookware range at www.MrDsCookware.com. See the back of the book for details.

Lining the tin: Cut two circles of baking paper to fit a cake tin (one for the base and one for the top) that will fit in your thermal cooker. Grease the tin and line the base with one circle.

Method

1. Prepare a cake/pudding tin* that fits into your Shuttle Chef by greasing the tin and lining the base with baking paper.
2. Sprinkle the bicarbonate of soda over the chopped dates and pour on the boiling water.
3. Add the butter and sugar and beat well.
4. Add a well beaten egg, then stir in the flour.
5. Lastly add in the vanilla essence and nuts.
6. Spoon into the cake/pudding tin* and smooth the surface.
7. Put the lid onto the cake/pudding tin* and clip down (If using a cake tin without a lid, cover with foil and tie securely with string).
8. Place the cake/pudding tin* inside the inner pot on a trivet.
9. Add enough boiling water to come ¾ the way up the side of the cake/pudding tin and bring back to the boil.
10. Turn down the heat to a low simmer.
8. Simmer gently with the lid on for 30 minutes.
6. Turn off the heat and transfer the inner pot into the vacuum-insulated outer container.
7. Close the lid and leave to cook for a minimum of 4 to 5 hours. Ideally the cake should be left to cook overnight.

Carrot Cake - serves 8 to 10

 A wonderfully moist Carrot Cake that is sure to become a favourite.

Ingredients

- **125ml of vegetable oil**
- **½ a cup of brown sugar**
- **3 large eggs**
- **1 cup of self raising flour**
- **½ cup of plain flour**
- **1 tsp of bicarbonate of soda**
- **2 tsp ground cinnamon**
- **2 medium carrots, grated**
- **½ cup pecans, chopped**
- **1 cup of sultanas**

Method

1. Beat the eggs and add the sugar and oil and continue beating until very frothy.
2. Sift together the flours, bicarbonate of soda and cinnamon.
3. Add the egg mixture to the flour and then stir in the grated carrot, pecans and sultanas
4. Put the mixture into a cake/pudding tin* that has been greased and lined with baking paper and cover with a round of baking paper.
5. Put the lid onto the cake/pudding tin* and clip down (If using a cake tin without a lid, cover with foil and tie securely with string)
6. Place the cake/pudding tin* inside the inner pot on a trivet.
7. Add enough boiling water to come ¾ the way up the side of the cake/pudding tin and bring back to the boil.
8. Turn down the heat to a low simmer.
8. Simmer gently with the lid on for 30 minutes.
6. Turn off the heat and transfer the inner pot into the vacuum-insulated outer container.
7. Close the lid and leave to cook for a minimum of 4 to 5 hours. Ideally the cake should be left to cook overnight.

---

* A Mr D's Cake/Pudding Tin is available from our cookware range at www.MrDsCookware.com. See the back of the book for details.

Lining the tin: Cut two circles of baking paper to fit a cake tin (one for the base and one for the top) that will fit in your thermal cooker. Grease the tin and line the base with one circle.

Boiled Fruit Cake - serves 8 to 10

A traditional slow cooked moist fruit cake.

Ingredients

- **375g mixed dried fruit**
- **¾ cup of brown sugar**
- **1 tsp mixed spice**
- **grated rind of an orange**
- **½ cup of water or orange juice**
- **¼ cup of whisky**
- **125g butter**
- **2 lightly beaten large eggs**
- **1 cup of self raising flour**
- **1 cup of plain flour**
- **½ tsp of bicarbonate of soda**

Method

1. Prepare the cake/pudding tin as described in the hints box below.
2. Place the dried fruit into a saucepan with the brown sugar, mixed spice, orange rind, water, whiskey and butter.
3. Bring the mixture to the boil and simmer uncovered for 5 minutes.
4. Allow the mixture to cool. This is very important as the eggs will cook if the mixture is hot.
5. Mix in the eggs.
6. Stir in the sifted flour and bicarbonate of soda.
7. Line a round cake/pudding tin* or Pyrex dish (one that fits nicely into the inner pot) with baking paper. If you butter the inside of the tin or Pyrex a circle of baking paper in the base will be enough.
8. Spoon the mixture into this prepared cake/pudding tin*.
9. Place the cake/pudding tin* inside the inner pot on a trivet.
10. Add enough boiling water to come ¾ the way up the side of the cake/pudding tin and bring back to the boil.
11. Put the lid on and turn down the heat. Simmer gently for 25 to 30 minutes.
12. Turn off the heat and transfer the inner pot into the vacuum-insulated outer container.
13. Close the lid and leave to cook for a minimum of 4 to 5 hours. Ideally the cake should be left to cook overnight.

* A Mr D's Cake/Pudding Tin is available from our cookware range at www.MrDsCookware.com. See the back of the book for details.

Lining the tin: Cut two circles of baking paper to fit a cake tin (one for the base and one for the top) that will fit in your thermal cooker. Grease the tin and line the base with one circle.

Ginger Cake - serves 8 to 10

 One of Nana's all time favourite cakes .

Ingredients

- 2 tbsp butter
- ½ cup brown sugar
- 1 tbsp golden syrup
- ½ tsp bicarbonate of soda
- 1 tsp vinegar
- 1 large egg
- 2 tbsp preserved ginger, chopped
- 1 flat tbsp ground ginger
- ½ cup of self raising flour
- ½ cup of plain flour

Optional - you can replace the ginger with the following:
- ½ cup of chopped dates or 2 tbsp of raisins and 2 tbsp of chopped nuts.

---

* A Mr D's Cake/Pudding Tin is available from our cookware range at www.MrDsCookware.com. See the back of the book for details.

Lining the tin: Cut two circles of baking paper to fit a cake tin (one for the base and one for the top) that will fit in your thermal cooker. Grease the tin and line the base with one circle.

Method

1. Prepare the cake/pudding tin as described in the hints box below.
2. Melt the butter, sugar and golden syrup over a low heat.
3. Stir in the bicarbonate of soda , vinegar and preserved ginger.
4. Allow the mixture to cool.
5. Add the lightly beaten egg.
6. Sift the dry ingredients and stir in lightly to the mixture.
7. Spoon the mixture into the prepared cake/pudding tin*.
8. Lay a round of baking paper on top of the cake mixture then cover the tin with the lid or a trimmed piece of eco-friendly foil tied with string.
9. Place a trivet in the inner pot and fill with hot water just over the level of the trivet.
10. Put the covered cake tin on the trivet and carefully adjust the hot water to come ¾ up the side of the cake tin or Pyrex.
11. Bring the water to the boil.
12. Put the pot lid on and turn down the heat. Simmer gently for 25 to 30 minutes.
13. Turn off the heat and transfer the inner pot into the vacuum-insulated outer container.
14. Close the lid and leave to cook for a minimum of 4 to 5 hours. Ideally the cake should be left to cook overnight.

Simple Chocolate Cake - *serves 8 to 10*

 Everyone loves a chocolate cake and they will love this one.

Ingredients

- 160g butter
- 1 cup castor sugar
- 4 tbsp cocoa
- 125ml boiling water
- 1 tbsp whisky (optional)
- 3 large eggs
- 1½ cups self raising flour
- 1 tsp cinnamon
- ½ tsp vanilla essence

Method

1. In a bowl melt the butter and sugar in boiling water. Stir in whisky (if using) and leave to cool.
2. Grease and line with baking paper, the base of a cake/pudding tin* or Pyrex dish that fits into the thermal cooker.
3. Mix into cooled mixture the three eggs that have been lightly beaten.
4. Fold in flour, cocoa, cinnamon. (sifted together).
5. Stir in vanilla essence.
6. Spoon the mixture into this prepared cake/pudding tin*.
7. Lay a round of baking paper on top of the cake mixture, put the lid on or cover the tin with a trimmed piece of eco-friendly foil tied with string.
8. Place a trivet in the inner pot and fill with hot water just over the level of the trivet.
9. Put the covered cake tin on the trivet and carefully adjust the hot water to come ¾ up the side of the cake tin or Pyrex.
10. Bring the water to the boil.
11. Put the lid on and turn down the heat. Simmer gently for 25 to 30 minutes.
12. Turn off the heat and transfer the inner pot into the vacuum-insulated outer container.
13. Close the lid and leave to cook for a minimum of 4 to 5 hours. Ideally the cake should be left to cook overnight.

* A Mr D's Cake/Pudding Tin is available from our cookware range at www.MrDsCookware.com. See the back of the book for details.

Bread & Scones

Bread made in a thermal cooker is moist and keeps very well. By using the no knead methods bread making is so easy.

Doris Grant's No Knead Bread

 This recipe was developed by Doris Grant as a fool-proof way to make wholesome bread during the rationing of WW2.

Ingredients

- 125g strong white bread flour, plus extra for dusting
- 125g strong wholemeal flour
- 1 tsp salt
- 5gm fast-action dried yeast
- 3/4 tbsp clear honey
- 175ml warm water
- butter or spread to grease the tin

Method

1. Cut a parchment (baking paper) base lining for the bread tin. Grease the tin, not forgetting the lid. Place the cut out parchment into the base.
2. Sift the flours into a large bowl and reserve the grain – the brown bits that are too big to fit through the sieve.
3. Add the salt and yeast and mix well.
4. Make a hole in the centre and pour in the honey and slightly warmed water.
5. Mix well with a wooden spoon to form a smooth dough.
6. Dust your hands with flour and remove the dough. Shape the dough to fit the greased bread tin and place it in. Dust the top with the grain husks that you sieved earlier.
7. Put the lid on the tin. Place a trivet in the inner pot, add 1 cup of boiling water and put the bread tin on the trivet. Put the inner pot into the insulated outer container and shut the lid. (If at home you can use the airing cupboard.)
8. Leave for 45 to 50 minutes to rise.
9. Once risen, remove the inner pot from the outer container. Add boiling water until the water comes about 3/4 of the way up the side of the bread tin.
10. Put the inner pot on a heat source and bring gently back to the boil.
11. Once boiling turn the heat down and simmer for 15 to 20 minutes with the inner pot lid on.
12. Turn off the heat. Place the inner pot into the insulated outer container, shut the lid and leave to thermal cook without power for a minimum of four hours. It can be left overnight.
13. Once cooked remove the tin from the inner pot, take off the lid, and after a few minutes run a knife carefully around the edge of the bread and turn out onto a rack.

* A Mr D's Bread Tin is available from our cookware range at www.MrDsCookware.com. See the back of the book for details.

Golden Syrup Scones

 A favourite winter dessert that is easily made.

Ingredients

- 1¾ cups of self raising flour
- 1 tbsp butter
- 1 tbsp castor sugar
- ½ tsp of cinnamon
- 2 tbsp golden syrup
- 1 large egg, lightly beaten
- 30ml of milk

Method

1. Grease a stainless steel cake/pudding tin* that will fit into the Thermal Cooker inner pot.
2. Sift the flour into a bowl and rub in the butter.
3. Mix in the sugar and cinnamon.
4. Add the syrup with the egg and sufficient milk to make a soft dough.
5. Knead gently.
6. Roll out to fit your tin.
7. With a knife, cut through the dough to make even sized scones (approximately 8).
8. Gently transfer these into the tin.
9. Put on the lid, or if using a non lidded tin cover with eco-friendly foil.
10. Place a trivet in the inner pot and fill with hot water just over the level of the trivet.
11. Put the covered cake tin on the trivet and carefully adjust the hot water to come ¾ up the side of the cake tin.
12. Bring the water to the boil.
13. Put the lid on and turn down the heat. Simmer gently for 15 to 20 minutes.
14. Turn off the heat and transfer the inner pot into the vacuum-insulated outer container.
15. Close the lid and leave to cook for a minimum of 30 minutes.

* A Mr D's Bread Tin is available from our cookware range at www.MrDsCookware.com. See the back of the book for details.

Wholemeal Bread

 A very simple standard recipe bread mix that produces excellent results.

Ingredients

- 6g of dry yeast
- $^3/_4$ cup wholemeal flour
- $^3/_4$ cup plain white flour
- 1 tsp brown sugar
- $^1/_2$ tbsp vegetable oil
- 140ml warm water
- sesame seeds

Method

1. Mix the dry ingredients together in a bowl.
2. Add the oil and water and mix to form a soft dough.
3. Turn onto a lightly floured board and knead for about 10 minutes until smooth and elastic.
4. Cover with a clean damp cloth and allow to rise in a warm place for about 20 - 30 minutes.
5. Turn the dough over and shape it gently and fit in a greased bread tin* (the one from Mr D's cookware would be ideal).
6. Sprinkle with sesame seeds.
7. Put on the lid, or if using a non lidded tin cover with eco-friendly foil.
8. Place the tin inside the inner pot on a trivet.
9. Add enough boiling water to come ¾ the way up the side of the cake/pudding tin.
6. Bring to the boil.
7. Turn down the heat and simmer gently for 15 to 20 minutes with the lid on.
8. Turn off the heat and transfer the inner pot into the vacuum-insulated outer container.
9. Close the lid and leave to cook for a minimum of 4 hours. If you leave it longer it will not matter.

* A Mr D's Bread Tin is available from our cookware range at www.MrDsCookware.com. See the back of the book for details.

Basic Recipes

Master Stock

 This aromatic, reusable stock is used a lot in Cantonese cooking. Once the base stock has been prepared it is then used as a poaching or braising liquid for chicken, duck or pork.

Ingredients

- 2 litres of water
- 4 cloves garlic, sliced
- 4 cm piece of ginger, sliced
- 6 spring onions or shallots, chopped in half
- 1 cinnamon stick
- 3 star anise
- 3 pieces of dried orange peel. You can buy this at an Asian supermarkets or peel an orange (without the white pith as this is bitter) and dry it slowly in the oven on a very low heat.
- 250ml light soy sauce
- 250ml Shoaxing wine (Chinese cooking wine)
- 75g Chinese yellow rock sugar (granulated sugar can be used)

Method

1. Fill a saucepan with the water.
2. Add the sliced garlic, ginger and spring onions or shallots, followed by the aromatics.
3. Add the light soy, Shaoxing wine and Chinese rock sugar.
4. Bring to the boil and taste the stock for balance of flavours. If it requires more salt, add a little more soy sauce.
5. Continue to boil for 3 to 4 minutes skimming the surface of impurities if needed.
6. Put on the lid, turn off the heat and transfer the inner pot into the vacuum-insulated outer container.
7. Close the lid and leave to cook for a minimum of 1 hour. If you leave it longer it will not matter.
8. Allow the stock to cool, if not using straight away, strain it through a fine sieve and refrigerate until needed.

SAFETY NOTE: After use, if the master stock is not being immediately reused it should be boiled, skimmed, strained and cooled quickly to minimise the potential for bacterial growth. The stock should then be refrigerated or frozen until required. Refrigerated stocks may be kept for up to three days, while frozen stocks may be kept for up to a month. If the stock is to be kept longer it must be boiled before being reused.

Master stock, once cooled, strained and refrigerated can be used again and again. Replenish the stock with fresh garlic, ginger, shallots and aromatics each time you use it and the flavour will continue to intensify in strength and flavour.
This stock can also be frozen.

Vegetable Stock

 I don't add salt to stocks until I use them. The stock can then be used with or without something that is already salted.

Ingredients

- 2 tbsp virgin olive oil
- 1 onion with skin, coarsely chopped
- 1 small carrot with skin, coarsely chopped
- 2 whole cloves of garlic
- 2 stick of celery, thickly sliced
- 1 bay leaf
- 2.25 litres of water
- 6 stalks parsley, coarsely chopped
- 1 tsp black peppercorns

Method

1. Add all the ingredients to the inner pot.
2. Bring to the boil.
3. Turn down the heat and simmer for 10 minuets.
4. Turn off the heat, put on the lid and transfer the inner pot into the vacuum-insulated outer container.
5. Close the lid and leave to cook for a minimum of 1 hour. If you leave it longer it will not matter.
6. Strain the stock through a fine sieve and allow it to cool. If not using straight away, refrigerate or freeze it until needed.

Beef Stock

 I don't add salt to stocks until I use them. The stock can then be used with or without something that is already salted.

Ingredients

- 1kg beef bones
- 250g beef brisket
- 2 brown onions, including skin halved
- 1 large carrot, trimmed but unpeeled and coarsely chopped
- 2 stalks celery, coarsely chopped
- 1 swede, coarsely chopped
- 2 tsp black peppercorns
- Water to cover

Method

1. Add all the ingredients to the inner pot.
2. Bring to the boil and skim off any impurities on the surface
3. Continue to boil for 3 to 4 minutes skimming the top if needed.
4. Put on the lid, turn off the heat and transfer the inner pot into the vacuum-insulated outer container.
5. Close the lid and leave to cook for a minimum of 2 to 3 hours. If you leave it longer it will not matter.
6. Strain the stock through a fine sieve and allow it to cool. If not using straight away, refrigerate or freeze it until needed.
7. Taste the stock and adjust the seasoning if needed.

Chicken Stock

 I don't add salt to stocks until I use them. The stock can then be used with or without something that is already salted.

Ingredients

- 750g chicken bones
- 250g chicken giblets
- 3 litres of water
- 1 onion including skin, coarsely chopped
- 1 large carrot, trimmed but unpeeled and coarsely chopped
- 1 tsp of black peppercorns

Method

1. Add all the ingredients to the inner pot.
2. Bring to the boil and skim off any impurities on the surface
3. Continue to boil for 3 to 4 minutes skimming the top if needed.
4. Put on the lid, turn off the heat and transfer the inner pot into the vacuum-insulated outer container.
5. Close the lid and leave to cook for a minimum of 2 to 3 hours. If you leave it longer it will not matter.
6. Strain the stock through a fine sieve and allow it to cool. If not using straight away, refrigerate or freeze it until needed.
7. Taste the stock and adjust the seasoning if needed.

Fish Stock

 I don't add salt to stocks until I use them. The stock can then be used with or without something that is already salted.

Ingredients

- **1.25kg seafood trimmings such as heads, tails, prawn heads etc.**
- **1 onion, with skin, coarsely chopped**
- **1 small carrot, with skin, coarsely chopped**
- **2 sticks of celery, thickly sliced**
- **1 bay leaf**
- **1 cm of ginger, squashed**
- **2.5 litres of water**
- **2 tbsp white wine vinegar**

Method

1. Add all the ingredients to the inner pot.
2. Bring to the boil and skim off any impurities on the surface
3. Continue to boil for 3 to 4 minutes skimming the top if needed.
4. Put on the lid, turn off the heat and transfer the inner pot into the vacuum-insulated outer container.
5. Close the lid and leave to cook for a minimum of 2 to 3 hours. If you leave it longer it will not matter.
6. Strain the stock through a fine sieve and allow it to cool. If not using straight away, refrigerate or freeze it until needed.
7. Taste the stock and adjust the seasoning if needed.

Perfect Rice

 This is my method of getting rice cooked perfectly every time.

Ingredients

- ½ cup of log grain rice per person
- 2 thirds cup of boiling water per ½ cup of rice
- ¼ tsp salt per cup of water

(for 4 helpings, 2 cups rice and 3 cups water)

Method

Cooking Rice

1. Add the rice, water and salt to a saucepan with a lid.
2. Bring to the boil.
3. Give a stir with a fork to break up any lumps.
4. Turn off the heat and put the lid on the pan.
5. Leave for 20—30 minutes when the rice will be cooked perfectly.
6. Fluff up with a fork before serving.

To Thermal Cook Rice in Mr D's Top Pot

To thermal cook rice (for up to 4 servings) at the same time as the main dish, use the lidded top pot for Mr D's cookware range.

1. Put the rice, water and salt in the top pot and stir to distribute the grains in the water.
2. Bring to the boil.
3. Give a stir with a for to break up any lumps.
4. Turn off the heat and carefully lift the top pot (be careful as the handles may be hot) and place it in the top of the inner pot above the main meal.
5. Leave the rice cooking for the length of time stated in the main meal recipe.
6. Before serving fluff up the rice.

Tomato Sauce

 Your thermal cooker is ideal for making homemade tomato sauce.

Ingredients

- 1 medium onion, finely chopped
- 1 celery stick, finely chopped
- 1 carrot, finely chopped
- 25g butter
- 2 cloves of garlic, crushed
- 2 x 396g cans of chopped tomatoes
- ½ tsp of basil
- ½ tsp of oregano
- ½ tsp ground bay leaves
- 150ml red wine or vegetable stock
- salt and pepper

Method

1. Put the inner pot on a medium heat and add the butter.
2. When the butter is melted add the onion, celery, carrots and garlic.
3. Cook until the onions are soft and then add the tomatoes, herbs and wine or stock.
4. Bring to the boil and boil for 3 to 4 minutes.
5. Put on the lid, turn off the heat and transfer the inner pot into the vacuum-insulated outer container.
6. Close the lid and leave to cook for a minimum of 2 hours. If you leave it longer it will not matter.
7. Once ready blend either with a hand blender or put into a liquidiser then press through a sieve for a smooth sauce.
8. Check the seasoning and adjust if necessary.

Fresh Tomato Chutney

 The ideal accompaniment for any Indian curry but especially biryani.

Ingredients

- 1 small green chilli, (deseed and chop very finely)
- ½ medium onion, (chop finely) I prefer sweet red onion.
- 3 large or 4 medium tomatoes, (chopped)
- 1 tbsp vinegar
- 1 tsp sugar
- Good pinch salt

Method

1. Stir all ingredients together, cover and leave in a cool place for flavours to blend.

Preserved Lemons

 Preserved lemons, sold loose in the souks, are one of the indispensable ingredients of Moroccan cooking, used in fragrant lamb and vegetables tagines, recipes for chicken with lemons and olives, and salads.

Ingredients

- 8-10 lemons, scrubbed very clean
- ½ cup salt, more if needed
- Extra fresh squeezed lemon juice, if needed

Storage Jar: You will also need a 1 litre sterilised jar. A Kilner jar would be ideal.

Optional: You can add spices to the lemons for preserving - cloves, coriander seeds, peppercorns, cinnamon stick, bay leaf.

Method

1. Scrub the lemons and trim off the little rounded bit at the stem end if there's a hard little piece of the stem attached.
2. From the other end of the lemon, make a large cut by slicing lengthwise downward, stopping about 3 cm from the bottom, then making another downward slice at 90°, so you've incised the lemon with an cross shape.
3. Pack about 1 tablespoon of coarse salt into the lemon where you made the cross incision.
4. Put the salt-filled lemons into the sterilised jar, pressing them down firmly to get the juices flowing until the jar is full.
5. Top up with fresh lemon juice if required.
6. Seal the jar and let it sit at room temperature for a couple days turning it upside down occasionally.
7. After three days put the jar in the refrigerator. Turn it upside down occasionally, for at least 3 weeks, until lemon rinds soften.
8. They are then ready for use and can be kept in the fridge for up to 6 months. Remember to rinse before using to remove excess salt.

Index

Lamb 42 - 52

Beef 54 - 58

Pork 60 - 70

Vegetarian 72 -76

Conversion Chart ~ All conversions are rounded up or down as appropriate.

1 ounce = 28g
4 ounces = 112g
8 ounces = 225g
16 ounces = 450g/1lb
32 ounces = 900g = 2lbs
36 ounces = 1000g (1kg) = 2¼ lbs

¼ teaspoon = 1ml
½ teaspoon = 3mls
1 teaspoon = 6mls
1 tablespoon = 15mls = ½ fluid ounce
1 pint = 16 fluid ounces = 550mls
1 quarter = 32 fluid ounces = 1 litre
1 gallon = 128 fluid ounces = 3¾ litres

1 measuring cup = 8 fluid ounces
A coffee cup is usually smaller and holds about 6 fluid ounces

32° F = 0° C
122° F = 50° C
212° F = 100° C

American Cup Conversions
1 stick of butter = 4 ounces = 110g
1 cup of flour - 5 ounces = 140g
1 cup sugar = 8 ounces = 225g
1 cup of brown sugar = 6 ounces = 170g
1 cup of butter or margarine = 8 ounces - 225g
1 cup of raisins or sultanas = 7 ounces = 200g
1 cup of currants = 5 ounces = 140g
1 cup of ground almonds = 4 ounces = 110g
1 cup of rice/uncooked = 7 ounces = 200g
1 cup of grated cheese = 4 ounces = 110g

Mr D's 2nd Thermal Cookbook
"A Year of Thermal Cooking"

Mr D's eco-friendly Thermal Cooker	Model: Mr D's 3L Thermal Cooker
Capacity of the inner pot	3L
Temperature after 6 hours	65 to 70°C
Diameter of outer container	22cm x 28cm
Height of outer container	21.5cm

ACCESSORIES for Mr D's eco-friendly Thermal
Cooker - available from www.Mr D's Cookware.co.uk

Top Pot

Steamed Loaf Tin

Cake Tin

Trivet